The Transitional Generation

From Now to Eternity

Gary King

The Transitional Generation: From Now to Eternity

Copyright © 2019 Gary King

Printed in the United States of America.
All rights reserved.

ISBN: 978-1-7332884-0-8

Gary King
ARM Resources
Celina, Ohio
www.armresources.org

Unless otherwise noted, Scripture quotations are from the New King James Version (NKJV). Copyright © 1979, 1980, 1982 by Thomas Nelson, Inc.

Scripture quotations marked (KJV) are taken from King James Version. Public domain.

Scripture quotations from The ESV® Bible (The Holy Bible, English Standard Version®), copyright © 2001 by Crossway, a publishing ministry of Good News Publishers. Used by permission. All rights reserved.

All Rights Reserved. No part of this publication may be reproduced, stored in a retrieval system or transmitted in any form or by any means – electronic, mechanical, photocopy, recording or any other (except for brief quotations in printed reviews), without prior written permission of the author.

CONTENTS

Preface

We are living in a time when the number of views on eschatology are almost as numerous as there are church denominations (slight exaggeration). What is "Eschatology"? Webster's dictionary defines it as, "A branch of theology concerned with the final events in the history of the world. It would include various Christian doctrines such as The Second Coming, The Resurrection of the Dead, or The Last Judgment." Simply stated, it is the study of end-time events. Most who share their views on such, cite the Bible as their source and proof of the very doctrine they espouse.

Why are there so many views, if these views are based on the same book? Often, the reason for this is because the biblical view being espoused is not that of the one speaking, but rather the view of what he has heard another articulate. Many Christians simply parrot what they have been taught, assuming that it was biblically based, especially if the teacher is well-known. Attaching a Scripture to an opinion or view does not necessarily make it a biblical view. Most Christians, even many pastors, are not well-versed and studied on end-time events.

Why is it that so few have studied the Scriptures to ascertain what the Bible says about eschatology? Is it because they have been led to believe that eschatology is too deep to understand? Or is it because they have been taught that it is not really that important in our Christian walk? For whatever reason, the subject of eschatology is avoided by the majority of Christians, even by most pastors. Rarely is the last book of our Bible, the book of Revelation, used extensively as a part of the many sermons preached weekly from pulpits. It seems that the last book of the Bible is avoided like the plague. This most likely is the result of pastors not being confident or not feeling comfortable having to deal with the stir and the questions such teachings might generate.

Another book of the Bible that is seldom used in eschatological teachings today is the book of Daniel. Like the book of Revelation, this book too is cloaked with types and shadows and mysteries intentionally sealed by God until the time of the end. Much of the focus of *The Transitional Generation* will be on the book of Daniel and how it relates to the book of Revelation. Most people you talk to believe that we are fast approaching the end of this age. If that is true, should we not expect God to unseal the mysteries as He promised to do?

I trust that this book will serve to motivate you to be diligent in searching the Scriptures and inquiring inside the temple for the revelation of God concerning His view on eschatology. God does have a view. He has declared it in the Bible, which must mean it is important. If it is important to Him, should not be important to us also? Therefore, may we all be encouraged to study to show ourselves approved unto God, as workmen who do not need to be ashamed. Being ashamed of what? That is, being ashamed of not knowing what was important enough to God to include in our Bibles that we so dearly love and respect.

***

This book is a sequel to

The Terminal Generation

***

SECTION 1

The Revelations in Daniel

(End-Time Revelations of Daniel)

CHAPTER 1

SURVEY OF DANIEL

Introduction

Many people in our present day, whether religious or nonreligious, have a sense that we are about to face climatic, cataclysmic events. They realize that the course our world is on is not long sustainable. There seems to be an air of apprehension as well as fear and dread of what might be coming. Many have asked me the questions, "Do you think the end of the world is near?" and "How long do you think we have until the end?" and "What do you think is going to happen?" The subtitle for this book, *The Transitional Generation*, was inspired by these very often-asked questions. The caption I chose is, "From Now to Eternity."

In writing this book, it is my desire to share with you, the reader, a prophetic timeline of events that will occur between now and eternity. To do this, I will primarily use the writings of one Old Testament prophet, Daniel, and one New Testament apostle, John. I chose these because of their expertise and understanding concerning eschatology (the study of end-time events). In the case of Daniel, let's consider the fact he received two angelic visitations from Gabriel, an archangel, for the express purpose of giving him skill, knowledge, and understanding concerning the last days. In the case of John, not only was he an eyewitness of Jesus' most exhaustive, eschatological teaching on the Mount of Olives, but he was also caught up to heaven to receive the book of Revelation. There are many end-time prophecies in the Bible, but Daniel and the book of Revelation provide far more detail concerning the last days than do the other prophetic books.

I encourage those of you who have not read my book, *The Terminal Generation*, to do so before reading this book. This book is intended to be its sequel. In *The Terminal Generation*, I discussed in much detail the prophetic revelations recorded in the book of Revelation. I will spend much of my initial focus in this book on the revelations contained in the book of Daniel. After having done this, I will merge the revelations recorded in these two books to paint a prophetic picture of what the future holds. And now let us look at the revelations recorded in the book of Daniel.

The Book of Daniel

When reading the book of Daniel, you will find several revelations received by Daniel and various ruling kings during the time of Israel's seventy years of captivity. These revelations came in the form of different dreams, visions, and angelic visitations, which necessitated interpretations from heaven. Most of these revelations were given by God to provide insight into what would happen in the latter days. These revelations would span a time period from Daniel's day unto the end of this age. I have spoken to some of these in my earlier book, *The Terminal Generation*.

In this section I will, in varying degrees, look at these dreams and visions concerning end-time prophetic events, in the chronological order in which they were received. The only exception will be the revelation Daniel received as recorded in the ninth chapter of Daniel. This prophecy deals with a specified period in Israel's history that stops well short of the end of this age. I will cover this extensively in Section 2 of this book. It is important to note, for study purposes, that the book of Daniel was not written in chronological order. One can determine the chronology of Daniel by looking at the kings ruling in each chapter and the exact year of their reign. The chronological order of Daniel is chapters 1-4, 7-8, 5-6, 9, 11-12, 10.

A Survey of Daniel

Before we begin to look at the various revelations contained in Daniel, I think it best to do a brief survey of how this book is laid out. The first four chapters took place during the reign of King Nebuchadnezzar of Babylon while Israel was in captivity. In these chapters, the king had two dreams that troubled him so much that he could not sleep. What made things worse with the first dream is that, the morning after, the king could not remember the dream but found no relief from the distress of it. Daniel was the only one in all of his kingdom that could both tell him the dream and give its interpretation. Nebuchadnezzar was so grateful that he made Daniel the ruler over all the king's province and the chief governor over all the wise men of Babylon. The second dream the king had, about a great tree being cut down, troubled him also, but the king was able to remember the dream in great detail. When none in his kingdom could give the interpretation, he called for Daniel. Daniel was able to provide the interpretation concerning God's intention to humble the king until such time that he recognized that God, not Nebuchadnezzar, was the true Sovereign over all.

Chapters seven and eight reveal what comes next in the chronological order. These take place during the three-year reign of Belshazzar, the son of King Nebuchadnezzar. In these two chapters, Daniel has two dreams that deal with end-time prophecies. The first dream happened during the first year of this king's reign; the second occurred during the third year of Belshazzar's reign. I will cover these dreams in the next chapter of this book.

Chapter five picks up at the end of the third year of Belshazzar's reign in Babylon. In this chapter, the king saw a vision that greatly troubled him so much that his knees knocked against one another. Still, as in the past, none of the astrologers, magicians, or wise men could interpret that which came from the one true God. And again Daniel was called when all others failed. That very night King Belshazzar was killed, and his kingdom fell to the Medes and the Persians under King Darius and King Cyrus, per Daniel's interpretation of the handwriting on the wall. Interestingly, this story has spawned a much-quoted phrase describing when someone sees what the future holds. It is said of that person, "He could see the handwriting on the wall."

Chapter six deals with King Darius setting up the structure of his kingdom after his conquest of Babylon. He favored and promoted Daniel to a very high position in his government because of the divine spirit that was in and working through Daniel.

Next in order is chapter nine, which takes place during the first year of the reign of King Darius of Media. It was during this time that Daniel received revelation concerning the plight of Israel's future. He gained an understanding while studying the prophecies of Jeremiah that the time of Israel's captivity was near to being over. As he was praying and acknowledging Israel's culpability that led to their captivity, the angel Gabriel revisited Daniel to give him skill and understanding as to what the future would hold for the nation of Israel. Gabriel told Daniel that seventy weeks were determined on Israel during which six things would be accomplished. This is often referred to by biblical scholars as the Seventy Weeks of Daniel. I will go into much detail concerning this revelation in Section 2 of this book.

Chapter eleven opens with the phrase, "Also in the first year of Darius the Mede." This is a clear indication that the revelations recorded in this chapter also were received during the first year of the reign of Darius. These prophecies would focus on the various nations and their interactions with one another militarily both in the not-too-distant future and also in the last days of this age.

Chapter twelve picks up where chapter eleven leaves off and gives details of what will come to pass during the last seven years of this age and beyond.

Finally, in the chronology of Daniel, the tenth chapter takes place during the third year of the reign of King Cyrus of Persia, who was the successor to King Darius. As was prophesied, he was the greater of the two horns. This chapter records a vision about the last days that was seen by Daniel as he was beside the Tigris River with a group of men. Only Daniel saw the vision, but the others fled in fear to hide from the presence they sensed but could not see. This vision was the culmination of twenty-one days of fasting by Daniel during which he was inquiring of the Lord. I will speak to the particulars of this revelation in the ensuing chapters of this section.

CHAPTER 2

REVELATIONS IN DANIEL

Introduction

And now let us begin to look at the various revelations recorded in the book of Daniel. In this chapter, I will review briefly the revelations in Daniel, which I covered extensively in *The Terminal Generation*. I will write in greater detail about the revelations not addressed previously in the following chapters of this book.

Dream of the Great Image

In Daniel, chapter two, King Nebuchadnezzar had a dream that greatly troubled him. When he awoke the next day, he could not remember the dream. He summoned the magicians, astrologers, sorcerers, and wise men to reveal the dream and the interpretation, under penalty of death if they failed. When none could show the dream nor its interpretation, the King ordered the execution of all the wise men. When Daniel heard of it, he told the king's captain of the guard to inform the king that he would seek God and reveal the dream the next day. In a dream that very night, God revealed to Daniel the king's dream and also its interpretation. I will just do a short recap of the great image Nebuchadnezzar saw in his dream.

The head of this image was of gold and was a depiction of Nebuchadnezzar's empire. The breast and arms of silver depicted the empire of the Medes and Persians. The belly and thighs of bronze represented the Grecian empire under Alexander the Great. The legs of iron were a depiction of the Roman empire. The fifth empire was comprised of two feet and ten toes of iron mixed with clay. This empire refers to the last-days worldwide empire of the antichrist and the false prophet. Finally, Daniel saw a stone cut out of the mountain of the Lord, without man's involvement. This stone will crush all of these kingdoms and will become an everlasting kingdom on this earth.

Dream of the Great Tree

In chapter four, Nebuchadnezzar receives a dream about a tree that grows to a great height in the earth. Then a heavenly being comes and orders the tree to be cut down, leaving only its stump and roots. Daniel reveals that God is about to cut down the arrogance of the king until he humbles himself beneath the mighty hand of God and acknowledges God's unmatched greatness. Daniel prophesies that after the king's contriteness, God will restore him to his former glory. One year later, this prophecy began to take place.

A Vision of the Four Beasts

In chapter seven, during the first year of the reign of Belshazzar, Daniel has a vision of four beasts that rise up out of the sea, each being diverse from the other.

> [1]In the first year of Belshazzar king of Babylon, Daniel had a dream and visions of his head while on his bed. Then he wrote down the dream, telling the main facts. [2]Daniel spoke, saying, "I saw in my vision by night, and behold, the four winds of heaven were stirring up the Great Sea. [3]And four great beasts came up from the sea, each different from the other. [4]The first was like a lion, and had eagle's wings. I watched till its wings were plucked off, and it was lifted up from the earth and made to stand on two feet like a man, and a man's heart was given to it. [5]"And suddenly another beast, a second, like a bear. It was raised up on one side and had three ribs in its mouth between its teeth. And they said thus to it: 'Arise, devour much flesh!' [6]"After this, I looked, and there was another, like a leopard, which had on its back four wings of a bird. The beast also had four heads, and dominion was given to it. [7]"After this, I saw in the night visions, and behold, a fourth beast, dreadful and terrible, exceedingly strong. It had huge iron teeth; it was devouring, breaking in pieces, and trampling the residue with its feet. It was different from all the beasts that were before it, and it had ten horns.
>
> —Daniel 7:1-7

Many scholars identify these beasts as Babylon, Media and Persia, Greece, and Rome. Though I believe this to be true, I also think the first three beasts serve as a typological picture of what happens between the sixth world empire and the seventh. Notice that after the fall of Rome, there is no mention of a worldwide empire again until that of the beast of the last days. Though there were centuries of no world-dominant empires, there were significant empires established that had great influence on the earth. The four beasts mentioned here are a confirmation of the previous revelations recorded in Daniel as well as what was recorded by John in his revelation.

The first beast represented by the lion with the eagle's wings is Nebuchadnezzar, who was lifted up with pride, acclaiming himself as a deity until God clipped his wings and caused him to graze with the beasts of the field. After he was humbled, God caused him to stand up a mere man, now knowing that there is only one true Sovereign God.

The second beast was represented as a bear who was raised up higher on one side, having three ribs in his mouth. This speaks of the kingdom of the Medes and Persians with the second king, Cyrus being greater than the first king, Darius. The three ribs represent Media, Persia, and Babylon.

The third beast was like a four-headed leopard with four wings of a bird on its back. This is representative of the Grecian empire under Alexander the Great who, with his four generals, flew swiftly over the earth to conquer the empire of the Medes and Persians.

The fourth beast, who was more dreadful, terrible, and exceedingly stronger than the other three, will be reminiscent of the Roman empire described in Daniel, chapter two.

However, this fourth beast with its leader, the antichrist, will be different from its three predecessors in that this empire shall devour the whole earth as opposed to just having a significant impact.

> [23]"Thus he said: 'The fourth beast shall be a fourth kingdom on earth, which shall be different from all other kingdoms, and shall devour the whole earth, trample it, and break it in pieces. —Daniel 7:23

This means the first three were not considered worldwide empires like the fourth beast. John's revelation echoes this position in describing the seven worldwide empires represented by the seven-headed great red dragon.

> [9]"Here is the mind which has wisdom: The seven heads are seven mountains on which the woman sits. [10]There are also seven kings. Five have fallen, one is, and the other has not yet come. And when he comes, he must continue a short time. [11]The beast that was, and is not, is himself also the eighth, and is of the seven, and is going to perdition. —Revelation 17:9-11

From this Scripture, we can see that one of these seven empires with its king was, is not, and yet will come in the future. At the writing of this Scripture in 95 AD, the first five had come and gone, the sixth (Rome) was current, and the seventh was yet to come. This means that the one who was and currently is not, had to be one of the first five. Who could this king be? Let's consider a few passages from Daniel for clues as to the origin of the seventh king.

> [8]Therefore the male goat grew very great; but when he became strong, the large horn was broken, and in place of it four notable ones came up toward the four winds of heaven. [9]And out of one of them came a little horn which grew exceedingly great toward the south, toward the east, and toward the Glorious Land. [10]And it grew up to the host of heaven, and it cast down some of the host and some of the stars to the ground and trampled them. [11]He even exalted himself as high as the Prince of the host, and by him, the daily sacrifices were taken away, and the place of His sanctuary was cast down.
>
> —Daniel 8:8-11

Let me explain. The seventh head represents the empire of the beast and its leader (Antichrist). This leader does not emerge from the reconstituted Roman empire as many believe, but from the reconstituted Grecian empire, which was one of the first five. The first six world empires are separated from the seventh, which is to come, by a time span extending from the fall of the Roman empire in 476 AD until today. This final worldwide empire is described in the passage below.

> [2]Now the beast which I saw was like a leopard, his feet were like the feet of a bear, and his mouth like the mouth of a lion. The dragon gave him his power, his throne, and great authority. [3]And I saw one of his heads as if it had been mortally wounded, and his deadly wound was healed. And all the world marveled and followed the beast.
>
> —Revelation 13:2-3

When the leader of that empire comes, he will only last a short time before he is mortally wounded. However, he will raise from the dead and become the eighth and yet is also from one of the seven world empires, namely the fifth.

I believe the three beasts preceding the Roman empire are a type and shadow of the three that precede the empire of the beast. As these possess many characteristics of their respective predecessors (Babylon – Media/Persia – Greece), so does the beast and its leader, the Antichrist, have many of the same characteristics of the Roman empire.

Though there were centuries of no world-dominant empires, there were significant empires established that had great influence on the earth. I believe these beasts represent more than a mere repeat of the global empires of the Great Image and the four beasts found in Daniel. These are also representative of three of the most powerful empires that arise after the fall of Rome and before the rise of the empire of the beast.

I believe that the lion with eagle's wings represents the United Kingdom (the lion) and the United States (the eagle's wings plucked off of the lion's back). When the UK lost the US, her empire lost significant strength and operated like a mere man rather than a superpower in the world. I believe the bear represents Russia, who became one of the dominant world powers and devoured much flesh. The leopard represents Germany, who with lightning speed conquered many nations and threatened world domination. Although these three achieved significant status in the world, their dominion was not universal. Rome was the last of the worldwide empires. However, when it comes to the fourth beast, Daniel 7:23-25 makes it clear that this beast will not only be dominant in this natural world but also dominant in the spiritual world until the Ancient of Days brings His judgment to bear on this imposter.

> [23]"Thus he said: 'The fourth beast shall be a fourth kingdom on earth, which shall be different from all other kingdoms, and shall devour the whole earth, trample it and break it in pieces. [24]The ten horns are ten kings who shall arise from this kingdom. And another shall rise after them; he shall be different from the first ones and shall subdue three kings. [25]He shall speak pompous words against the Most High, shall persecute the Most High of God, and shall intend to change times and law. Then the saints shall be given into his hand for a time and times and half a time. —Daniel 7:23-25

This empire is none other than the Beast spoken of in Revelation, chapter thirteen. In this vision, Daniel sees that the saints will eventually prevail against the Beast, and the everlasting kingdom of God will reign over the whole earth. This is congruent with and reinforces the interpretation of the "Great Image" of Daniel, chapter two, which depicts God's kingdom destroying all of the nations of this world and becoming an everlasting kingdom.

> [11]"I watched then because of the sound of the pompous words which the horn was speaking; I watched till the beast was slain, and its body destroyed and given

> to the burning flame. [12]As for the rest of the beasts, they had their dominion taken away, yet their lives were prolonged for a season and a time. —Daniel 7:11-12

It is interesting to note from the above Scripture that the three beasts were obviously contemporaries of the fourth dreadful beast. Though the dominion of the first three beasts was taken away, they still continued to exist even after the fall of the fourth beast. This substantiates that the first three beasts were not referring only to the previous worldwide empires of Babylon, Media/Persia, and Greece, as many scholars insist.

Not only does chapter seven reveal four powerful empires that will have a significant impact on the world during the last days, but it also introduces one of the most important prophetic characters that will play a vital role in the lives of all the people who dwell on the earth during his short reign.

The first mention in the book of Daniel of the Antichrist, the leader of the final world empire, is found in Daniel 7:8.

> [8]I considered the horns, and, behold, there came up among them another little horn, before whom there were three of the first horns plucked up by the roots: and, behold, in this horn were eyes like the eyes of man, and a mouth speaking great things. —Daniel 7:8

The following verses in this chapter go back and forth between the kingdom of God and the kingdom of the Beast/Antichrist. These verses alternately describe what God and the Antichrist are going to do, according to Daniel's dream.

Even though Daniel saw that the reign of the Antichrist would be short-lived and that the kingdom of God would triumph over him, he was exceedingly grieved in his spirit and troubled by the impact of the Beast and the little horn. It prompted him to question a heavenly watcher who was actually in Daniel's dream as a bystander observing what Daniel was seeing. He quizzed this watcher about the fourth beast and the little horn who usurped power over three of the ten kings. This watcher answered Daniel's questions and gave him greater understanding concerning the dream. He made known to Daniel that the little horn/Antichrist would make war with the saints and prevail against them for three and a half years (time, times, and half a time). This period is referred to as the great tribulation in the Scriptures. As we explained in great depth in *The Terminal Generation*, the tribulation period is for the "saints," not the "aints." Yes, the church will be going through the great tribulation. It is God's means to test her, cleanse her, and mature her. She will, through much tribulation, enter the kingdom of God while on this earth and learn to overcome all adversity through faith. After God's purpose is accomplished in the saints, He convenes a court session and determines that the saints are ready to possess the kingdom. At that time, the saints shall take away the dominion of the Antichrist as well as consume and destroy the kingdom of the Beast forever. They will put all the enemies of God under His feet and make them His footstool. They then will inherit the kingdom of God and shall be given the dominion and greatness of all the kingdoms under the whole heaven. This inherited kingdom is described by God as being an everlasting kingdom.

CHAPTER 3

Revelations in Daniel 8

Introduction

The revelations of Daniel, chapters eight and eleven, add considerable detail about the little horn introduced in Daniel, chapter seven. The Antichrist is inarguably one of the most important biblical figures in all the Bible, especially concerning the last days. We must remember, this character gets his power from the great red dragon, who the Scriptures clearly define as being the devil. Even as Christ is the incarnation of God, I believe the Antichrist will be the incarnation of Satan himself. Satan has long been obsessed with counterfeiting that which God brings forth. There are only two real options in life, the true and the false. There were two trees, two vines, and two seeds from which all are begotten. The first is true and is of God, the Father of truth; the second is false and is of Satan, the father of lies. Jesus is the Tree of life, the true Vine, and the one Seed, born of a woman, that will overcome the seed of Satan. The incarnated seed of Satan will bring forth the most wicked, vile human being to ever exist on this earth! The Church would do well to not underestimate this evil one who is prophesied to come soon. If it were not for God shortening those days, even the very Elect would be deceived. Because of the importance of this figure, I will spend considerable time discussing his origin, the supernatural things he will accomplish during his reign, and his devastating end. Since chapters eight and eleven of Daniel contain so much information about the Antichrist, I will cover the visions of these two chapters in greater detail than the previous revelations which I discussed extensively in my last book.

Daniel, Chapter Eight

In this chapter, Daniel sees a vision while still being in captivity in Babylon during the third year of the reign of Belshazzar. He sees himself in the palace in Shushan, Persia, even before the Medes and Persians conquered the Babylonians. He saw what we now call history before it ever happened. In this vision, Daniel sees a ram with two horns (Medes and Persians) being attacked and conquered by a he-goat with one notable horn (Greece led by Alexander the Great). Soon afterward, the large, notable horn (Alexander) dies. His kingdom is divided up into four regions and governed by his four, notable generals as seen in verses 8 and 9.

> 8Therefore the he-goat waxed very great: and when he was strong, the great horn was broken; and for it came

> up four notable ones toward the four winds of heaven. 9And out of one of them came forth a little horn, which waxed exceeding great, toward the south, and toward the east, and toward the pleasant land. —Daniel 8:8-9

Verses eight and nine make it clear that from one of the four notable horns, a little horn will come forth. It is absolutely essential that one understands the transition that Daniel makes in the very next verse. In verse ten, the prophecy fast forwards to the end of the age, at which time the little horn (the Antichrist) will come forth from a leader that succeeds one of the four generals of Alexander's now divided empire. This leader will be the root from which a new branch (genealogy) will begin that leads to and concludes with the Antichrist. This little horn (Antichrist) will grow exceedingly great, even to be able to war against the host, the army of heaven. Not only will he be up to the task of fighting against angels, but it also says that he will be powerful enough to cast some of the heavenly army and angels to the ground and trample them. Again I remind you, Revelation thirteen says he gets his power from Satan, and we know that Satan can fight against angels. Daniel was told that one of Satan's princes (Prince of Persia) was able to withstand and block Gabriel from completing his assignment until Michael came with reinforcements. Though spiritual beings are eternal and cannot die, they apparently can be rendered unable to fight or even bound as are those fallen angels who are now chained in the bottomless pit. How all of this warfare works in the spiritual realm or what it looks like, I don't even want to venture a guess. I'll leave that to Hollywood. All I know is that much of this type of warfare is currently going on, and it is very real to those engaged in the conflicts. If we only knew how much this spiritual warfare affects our natural world, we would indeed take it far more seriously. It impacted Daniel then, and likewise us today.

Getting back to the little horn I described previously, he will become exceedingly powerful and will even exalt himself against Jesus, the Prince of the host. He will suppress the worship of the one true God by His people, and cast down God's sanctuary, which is His temple. It is essential to understand that in the days of the fulfillment of this prophecy, the temple of God is a building of living stones made without the hands of man. It is the Church of the Living God, as many New Testament Scriptures plainly state. He will also cast truth to the ground. He will do all of this in the face of God and His people and prosper for a short season.

> 10And it grew up to the host of heaven, and it cast down some of the host and some of the stars to the ground and trampled them. 11He even exalted himself as high as the Prince of the host, and by him, the daily sacrifices were taken away, and the place of His sanctuary was cast down. 12Because of transgression, an army was given over to the horn to oppose the daily sacrifices; and he cast truth down to the ground. He did all this and prospered. —Daniel 8:10-12

At this point in Daniel's vision, he sees a holy one asking a question of another holy one as to how long it would be until the saints of God are trampled underfoot (the great tribulation). The answer was, "Until two thousand three hundred days," after which the sanctuary (temple) would be cleansed.

> [13]Then I heard a holy one speaking; and another holy one said to that certain one who was speaking, "How long will the vision be, concerning the daily sacrifices and the transgression of desolation, the giving of both the sanctuary and the host to be trampled underfoot?"
> [14]And he said to me, "For two thousand three hundred days; then the sanctuary shall be cleansed."
>
> —Daniel 8:13-14

As to the 2,300-day time period, I believe it begins with what was being discussed in the vision at the moment the question was posed. Just before its asking, the conversation was about the beginning of the genealogy stemming from one of the four leaders of Alexander's divided empire from which a little horn, and eventually the Antichrist, would come. One of the leaders of the four regions will be the root that bears the branch that will culminate with the birth of the Antichrist.

However, figuring out which root and which branch initiates that genealogy is not a simple matter. Concerning the 2,300 days, it is of such prophetic importance that we must first establish a sufficient historical background from Daniel, chapter eleven, before attempting to interpret its meaning. We will explore this in greater detail in Section 4 of this book.

After seeing this vision, Daniel was seeking its meaning when suddenly Gabriel appeared and was told by a heavenly being to make Daniel understand the vision. Gabriel informed Daniel that the vision refers to the time of the end and that he was there to make Daniel know what shall happen in the latter time of indignation. He went on to say, "For at the appointed time the end shall be." The phrase, "At the appointed time" is *mow-ed* in the Hebrew language. It means an appointed time/season, a sacred/set feast or festival, an appointed sign or signal of a prophetic event yet to come. This word appears in five verses in Daniel. In each case, its use is about the appointed time of the end.

> [15]Then it happened, when I, Daniel, had seen the vision and was seeking the meaning, that suddenly there stood before me one having the appearance of a man. [16]And I heard a man's voice between the banks of the Ulai, who called, and said, "Gabriel, make this man understand the vision." [17]So he came near where I stood, and when he came I was afraid and fell on my face; but he said to me, "Understand, son of man, that the vision refers to the time of the end." [18]Now, as he was speaking with me, I was in a deep sleep with my face to the ground; but he touched me, and stood me upright. [19]And he said, "Look, I am making known to you what shall happen in the latter time of the indignation; for at the appointed time the end shall be. —Daniel 8:15-19

There is another element that clouds our ability to decipher not only the mystery of the 2,300 days but also the visions of Daniel. I speak of the instructions given by God to Daniel to stop pursuing greater understanding because the words are sealed until the time of the end. This literally makes a complete understanding of them impossible until God unseals it at the appointed time in the last days.

> 26And the vision of the evening and the morning which was told is true: wherefore shut thou up the vision; for it shall be for many days. —Daniel 8:26

> 8And I heard, but I understood not: then said I, O my Lord, what shall be the end of these things? 9And he said, Go thy way, Daniel: for the words are closed up and sealed till the time of the end. —Daniel 12:8-9

Does this mean we should not seek to understand? I don't think so. First of all, the wisdom of Proverbs 25:2 instructs us as follows, "It is the glory of God to conceal a matter, but the glory of kings is to search out a matter." Since my last name is "King," seeking is my destiny. Bad joke, I know. Seriously, I remind you that God has made all of His people to be kings and priests, therefore, be a seeker of that which God has concealed. Secondly, we may not know the exact moment God will unseal this mystery, but we do know that we are indeed at the beginning of the last days according to Jesus' own teaching. The Olivet Discourse, found in three of the four gospels, is where Jesus instructs us that when we see some of the signs begin to happen, we are to look up, for our redemption draws near. He goes on to say the generation that sees these start will not pass away until all of the signs are fulfilled. In Joel, chapters two and three, the prophet declares that in the days and time when the Holy Spirit is poured out on all flesh, the sun will be darkened and the moon will be turned to blood, would also be the same days and time when the Jews are restored to their land and their city. In other words, all these events are prophesied to happen in the same time period. Indeed the signs of the end are evident to those who are even somewhat spiritually alert. If indeed we are convinced we are in the last days, should we not be looking for the visions of Daniel to be unsealed?

Continuing in Daniel 8:20-25, Gabriel begins to explain the main characters and events of the vision.

> [20]The ram which you saw, having the two horns—they are the kings of Media and Persia. [21]And the male goat is the kingdom of Greece. The large horn that is between its eyes is the first king. [22]As for the broken horn and the four that stood up in its place, four kingdoms shall arise out of that nation, but not with its power. [23]"And in the latter time of their kingdom, When the transgressors have reached their fullness, A king shall arise, Having fierce features, Who understands sinister schemes. [24]His power shall be mighty, but not by his own power; He shall destroy fearfully, And shall prosper and thrive; He shall destroy the mighty, and also the holy people. [25]"Through his cunning He shall cause deceit to prosper under his rule, And he shall exalt himself in his heart. He shall destroy many in their prosperity. He shall even rise against the Prince of princes, But he shall be broken without human means. —Daniel 8:20-25

He identifies the ram with the two horns as being the kings of Media and Persia, which history shows to be Darius and Cyrus. The male goat is Greece and the great horn, its first king, was Alexander the Great. As I shared earlier, after Alexander's death, his empire was divided into four kingdoms with four leaders. Verse 23 catapults us over two thousand years ahead to a time when transgressors will have filled the cup of abominations to overflowing. Look at what is happening in all the societies around the world today. Sin has reached the same epic proportions as was evident in the days of Noah and in the days of Lot in Sodom. As the judgment of God followed His repeated warnings in those days, so it will come soon and suddenly to those who do not heed the warning in these final days of this age. It is during this type of morally bankrupt environment that the rise of the Antichrist will take place. He will have fierce features and who understands sinister schemes. He shall have mighty power to destroy, prosper, and thrive. He shall destroy that which is mighty and also the holy people through his cunning. Deceit will flourish under his rule, and he will exalt himself above all. However, he will be divinely broken and cast into the Lake of Fire.

After the vision was finished and Daniel was seeking its meaning, he received a vision of Gabriel standing beside him. Then he heard a voice telling Gabriel to make Daniel understand the vision. Daniel was so fearful that he fell on his face. The angel tells Daniel that the vision refers to the time of the end when an evil king shall arise who shall be mighty but not by his own natural power. He shall destroy the mighty and also the holy ones of God. He shall even rise up against the Prince of princes, but he will be broken by God alone. The angel again reiterates to Daniel that this vision refers to a time many days in the future. Therefore, we should not treat this passage of Scripture primarily as a history lesson about rulers from the Persian or Greek empires. God's primary intention of giving this revelation is that it not be historical but rather eschatological.

> 23"And in the latter time of their kingdom, when the
> transgressors have reached their fullness, a king shall
> arise, having fierce features, who understands sinister
> schemes. 24His power shall be mighty, but not by his
> own power; he shall destroy fearfully, and shall prosper
> and thrive; he shall destroy the mighty, and also the holy
> people. 25"Through his cunning, he shall cause deceit to
> prosper under his rule; and he shall exalt himself in his
> heart. He shall destroy many in their prosperity. He shall
> even rise against the Prince of princes, but he shall be
> broken without human means. 26"And the vision of the
> evenings and mornings which was told is true; there-
> fore seal up the vision, for it refers to many days in the
> future." —Daniel 8:23-26

Our prayer should be, "Lord, open the seals on these visions."

CHAPTER 4

REVELATIONS IN DANIEL 11

Introduction

In chapter eleven, Daniel receives another vision, which was given by God to expand on the previous vision of chapter eight. The fact that God would do this speaks to how vital He feels the content of this chapter is.

Remember, the first vision was about the beginning of a genealogy that would lead up to and conclude with the rise, reign, and fall of the Antichrist. This vision prophesies in great depth about many specific events that would occur and the major characters that would participate in these events before the end of the age. Everything that Daniel prophesied pertained to future happenings. Today, much of what was future for Daniel is history for us. A quick study of historical records is shocking because of the precise accuracy of what Daniel foretold. The historical confirmation of this prophecy's detail should convince even the skeptic that the rest of the vision will undoubtedly play out exactly as was prophesied. It raises the question, "Why would God have Daniel do this?" I believe the reason God gave such accurate detail about historical events before they happened was to prove the validity of the prophetic word that is yet to happen in our day. In addition to stirring up faith, the details will aid us in knowing the times and seasons that are upon us and also what we should do in preparing for these times. The fact that the Scriptures provide so much detail would lead one to believe that God's end-game is not to completely hide this information but instead make it mystically obscure to encourage one to search its unveiling.

In the following pages of this chapter, I will share a brief historical outline of what is being prophesied by Daniel in chapter eleven. For inquiring minds who want to know more details, there is much historical information available to be studied. Part of what Daniel foretold has already happened and is recorded. Part of what he foresaw has not yet happened and is end-time prophecy. My intention for the following outline is that your faith might be built up to believe that what is yet to happen will occur with the same degree of accuracy as that which has already happened. And now, let us begin our history lesson.

Daniel, Chapter Eleven

Daniel receives this revelation in the first year of King Darius, the Mede. In this chapter, Daniel begins to encourage the king by sharing the revelation he had received concerning the future of the kingdom of the Medes and Persians and beyond. God prophesies through Daniel that there would be three kings after Darius and even a fourth king who would be the greatest of them all. History records the three kings to be Cyrus, Cambyses I, and Darius Hystaspes. The fourth king, who is the greatest of the four following Darius, is Xerxes. Daniel prophesies this fourth king would eventually go to war against the king of Greece and be defeated.

> [2]And now I will tell you the truth: Behold, three more
> kings will arise in Persia, and the fourth shall be far richer
> than them all; by his strength, through his riches, he shall
> stir up all against the realm of Greece. [3]Then a mighty
> king shall arise, who shall rule with great dominion, and
> do according to his will. [4]And when he has arisen, his
> kingdom shall be broken up and divided toward the
> four winds of heaven, but not among his posterity nor
> according to his dominion with which he ruled; for his
> kingdom shall be uprooted, even for others besides
> these. —Daniel 11:2-4

Notice that these verses are talking about the same content as the vision in Daniel, chapter eight. Verse four describes once again the rise of Alexander the Great, his death, and his kingdom being divided up into four regions (Greece, Asia Minor, Syria, and Egypt). These regions will be ruled not by his posterity but by others. We know these others to be four generals who emerged after much infighting following the death of Alexander. The four were Lysimachus of Greece, Cassander of Asia Minor, Seleucus of Syria, and Ptolemy of Egypt. Let us continue a verse by verse outline.

The following passages often speak about the king of the South and the king of the North. Determining the identities of these kings is not as mystical as some scholars try to make it. Simply stated, the kings of the North and South were identified by their geographical positions relative to Jerusalem at the time of the fulfillment of the said historical or prophetic events. For example, when Daniel 11:5 took place, the kingdom immediately to the north of Jerusalem was Syria led by Seleucus. The kingdom directly to the south of Jerusalem was Egypt led by Ptolemy I. It is essential to take note that the borders of the kingdoms immediately north and south of Jerusalem changed often throughout the years as also did their respective leaders. Therefore, the defined boundaries and leaders of each varied according to the reality that existed at the time of the unfolding of each prophesied event. This is critical to remember when we move from examining the facts of historical events to considering the possibilities of what might be at the fulfillment of prophetic events. As these unfold, the king of the North will be the leader of the first viable kingdom to the north of Jerusalem, and in like manner, the king of the South will be the first viable leader of the kingdom immediately to the south of Jerusalem. Initially, the king of the South (Ptolemy) became the strongest of the four. He has a general under him by the name of Seleucus who he sent to conquer Syria for him. However, when Seleucus took control over Syria, he ruled over it himself instead of bringing it under the reign of Ptolemy. The dominion of Seleucus became greater than that of Ptolemy, yet they remained friends. However, when their children, Ptolemy I and Antiochus I, succeeded them to their thrones, the relationship that their fathers had deteriorated.

> [5]"Also the king of the South shall become strong, as well as one of his princes; and he shall gain power over him and have dominion. His dominion shall be a great dominion. —Daniel 11:5

After the death of the king of the South (Ptolemy I) and the king of the North (Antiochus I), there began to be much strife between the two empires and their sons who succeeded them, Ptolemy II and Antiochus II. This led to a series of six wars between the King of the South (Egypt) and the King of the North (Syria).

After some time, they made an alliance with one another when Ptolemy II gave his daughter, Bernice, to marry Antiochus II. So Antiochus II put away his wife and son (Laodice, and their son, Seleucus II) and married Bernice. After Ptolemy II died, Antiochus II divorced Bernice and remarried his former wife, Laodice. She, being bitter, had Bernice and her child with Antiochus II killed. Later she poisoned Antiochus II and appointed their son, Seleucus II, to be the king. History explains the meaning of verse six when Bernice nor Antiochus II retained their power, but were given up to death along with her escort from Egypt.

> [6]And at the end of some years they shall join forces, for the daughter of the king of the South shall go to the king of the North to make an agreement; but she shall not retain the power of her authority, and neither he nor

> his authority shall stand; but she shall be given up, with those who brought her, and with him who begot her, and with him who strengthened her in those times.
> —Daniel 11:6

Following this murderous betrayal, Ptolemy III sought revenge. The phrase, "A branch from her root," in the following verse is about Bernice's brother, Ptolemy III. He attacked the king of the North, Seleucus II, and returned to Egypt with great spoil. Afterward, Seleucus II mounted a counter-attack, recapturing northern Syria and Phoenicia, but was finally turned back in Egypt. They then made a peace treaty which lasted almost twenty years until they both died and were succeeded by their respective sons, Ptolemy IV and Seleucus III.

> [7]But from a branch of her roots, one shall arise in his place, who shall come with an army, enter the fortress of the king of the North, and deal with them and prevail.
> [8]And he shall also carry their gods captive to Egypt, with their princes and their precious articles of silver and gold; and he shall continue more years than the king of the North. [9]Also the king of the North shall come to the kingdom of the king of the South, but shall return to his own land. —Daniel 11:7-9

Ptolemy III died in 222 BC, and Seleucus II died in 225 BC, which satisfies verse 8 that says the king of the South shall continue more years than the king of the North. After Seleucus II died, his two sons, Seleucus III, and Antiochus III stirred up strife and came against Ptolemy IV of Egypt.

Seleucus III only reigned three years until his death and was succeeded by his brother, Antiochus III, who became known as Antiochus the Great.

> [10]However, his sons shall stir up strife, and assemble a multitude of great forces; and one shall certainly come and overwhelm and pass through; then he shall return to his fortress and stir up strife. —Daniel 11:10

Ptolemy IV was enraged at the violation of the peace treaty and marched against the king of the North, Antiochus III. Ptolemy defeated the vast multitude of the Syrian army and, being lifted up with pride, he destroyed many Jews in the Holy Land in his return to Egypt. Approximately fourteen years later, Ptolemy IV died in 204 BC suddenly and mysteriously. He was replaced by his son, Ptolemy V, who was just a young lad. Antiochus the Great, seizing this opportunity, amassed an even greater army than before, laid siege on, and recaptured the holy land. No one was able to withstand him.

> [11]"And the king of the South shall be moved with rage, and go out and fight with him, with the king of the North, who shall muster a great multitude; but the multitude shall be given into the hand of his enemy. [12]When he has taken away the multitude, his heart will be lifted up; and he will cast down tens of thousands, but he will not prevail. [13]For the king of the North will return and muster a multitude greater than the former, and shall certainly come at the end of some years with a great army and much equipment. [14]"Now in those times, many shall rise up against the king of the South.

> Also, violent men of your people shall exalt themselves
> in fulfillment of the vision, but they shall fall. [15]So the
> king of the North shall come and build a siege mound,
> and take a fortified city, and the forces of the South shall
> not withstand him. Even his choice troops shall have no
> strength to resist. [16]But he who comes against him shall
> do according to his own will, and no one shall stand
> against him. He shall stand in the Glorious Land with
> destruction in his power. —Daniel 11:11-16

Antiochus the Great had ambitions to expand his empire to the coastlands of Asia Minor and Greece to re-establish the Alexandrian empire. Rather than having a war on two fronts, he devised a plan to finish his conquest of Egypt through deceit. He gave his daughter, Cleopatra I, to be married to Ptolemy V to form an alliance in 195 BC. After the marriage, Antiochus launched his campaign to conquer the coastlands. The next five years were marked with great success. Also at this time, the Roman empire was rising to great power. Seeking to fortify his position against Rome, Antiochus sought the help of his daughter, Cleopatra. However, she aligned herself with her husband and Rome instead. The Romans proceeded to soundly defeat Antiochus when he attacked Roman-occupied Greece. Rome pursued him, recaptured Asia Minor, and drove him back to his own fortress in Syria. Rome then forced Antiochus to surrender his navy, his 600-elephant army brigade, and twenty choice hostages as a ransom. Included in the hostages was his younger son, Antiochus IV, who spent his formative years being groomed in the Roman court with its culture. In addition to all of this, he had to pay a hefty financial penalty each year to Rome as war reparations. Desperate to raise the money to pay the penalty, he raised the taxes on his people. In his desperation, he also raided a pagan temple in his own country and was killed by the local people.

> [17]"He shall also set his face to enter with the strength of his whole kingdom, and upright ones with him; thus shall he do. And he shall give him the daughter of women to destroy it, but she shall not stand with him or be for him. [18]After this, he shall turn his face to the coastlands and shall take many. But a ruler shall bring the reproach against them to an end, and with the reproach removed, he shall turn back on him. [19]Then he shall turn his face toward the fortress of his own land, but he shall stumble and fall, and not be found.
>
> —Daniel 11:17-19

After the death of Antiochus the Great, he was succeeded by his first-born son, Seleucus IV, who reigned for twelve years. At this time, Rome freed his brother, Antiochus IV, who was taken as one of the twenty hostages, in exchange for Seleucus IV's son, Demetrius, who was heir to his throne. To finance his royal lifestyle and pay the Roman penalty, Seleucus IV sent tax collectors to the Holy Land to extract money and loot the temple of its treasures. At the end of his short reign, he was poisoned by one of his own trusted officials.

> [20]"There shall arise in his place one who imposes taxes on the glorious kingdom, but within a few days he shall

> be destroyed, but not in anger or in battle.
>
> —Daniel 11:20

The following verses describe the rise to power of a vile person who was not a part of the royal succession but gained the throne peacefully through flattery, deceit, and treachery. History records this person to be Antiochus IV, later known as Antiochus Epiphanies IV. Remember he was groomed by Rome, probably to place one of their own in the Seleucid empire to ensure continued control. However, he had his sights on controlling Egypt after Ptolemy V dies. Keep in mind that he was the brother of Cleopatra I, who was married to Ptolemy V. Antiochus IV made a peace treaty with Ptolemy VI and came down to Egypt with a small army to celebrate his cousin's coronation. While there, he undermined Ptolemy VI's government by bribing officials in the Egyptian political system. This was tactically crucial when he eventually came down with a mighty army against the king of the South. I believe what he did, and the way he did it, represents a typological fulfillment of the little horn who becomes the Antichrist at the end of the age.

> 21And in his place shall arise a vile person, to whom they
> will not give the honor of royalty; but he shall come in
> peaceably, and seize the kingdom by intrigue. 22With
> the force of a flood they shall be swept away from
> before him and be broken, and also the prince of the
> covenant. 23And after the league is made with him, he
> shall act deceitfully, for he shall come up and become
> strong with a small number of people. 24He shall enter
> peaceably, even into the richest places of the province;

> and he shall do what his fathers have not done, nor his forefathers: he shall disperse among them the plunder, spoil, and riches; and he shall devise his plans against the strongholds, but only for a time. —Daniel 11:21-24

Wanting to expand his empire, Antiochus IV stirred up animosities with the king of the South when he attacked and destroyed Egyptian held Jerusalem. He then was emboldened to attack Ptolemy VI. Though the army of the king of the South was large and powerful, it was not able to stand against the army of the North because of the pre-arranged plots devised against him by Antiochus IV. He was defeated from within by those he trusted, who ate at his table. The two kings then met at a supposed peace table to end the animosities, but they both were bent on evil and spoke lies to one another. Disappointed by the lack of success, Antiochus IV returned to his own land, and on the way, he took out his frustrations by raining destruction on Israel and, in particular, the city of Jerusalem. Israel was often caught in the angry crossfire by both parties in the Syrian/Egyptian wars.

> 25"He shall stir up his power and his courage against the king of the South with a great army. And the king of the South shall be stirred up to battle with a very great and mighty army; but he shall not stand, for they shall devise
> plans against him. 26Yes, those who eat of the portion of
> his delicacies shall destroy him; his army shall be swept
> away, and many shall fall down slain. 27Both these kings'
> hearts shall be bent on evil, and they shall speak lies at the same table; but it shall not prosper, for the end will
> still be at the appointed time. 28While returning to his

> land with great riches, his heart shall be moved against the holy covenant; so he shall do damage and return to his own land. —Daniel 11:25-28

Two times Antiochus IV tried to bring Egypt under the dominion of his empire. Each of these was a part of the sixth Syrian war with Egypt. Though he had limited success both times, he never entirely accomplished his goal. The sovereign God had predetermined that this goal would not be achieved by the king of the North until the appointed time at the end of this age. However, there will be a seventh and final war between the king of the North and the king of the South. This war will not be like the first or second attempts by Antiochus IV (the former or the latter to be seen in verse 29), for God has reserved that victory to be accomplished by the Antichrist (little horn) at the time of the end.

In the remaining verses of chapter eleven, Daniel continues the saga of this conflict between the king of the North and the king of the South. He began with Antiochus IV's last effort to defeat the king of the South and concluded with one last attempt by the Antichrist at the appointed time. I believe God intended that this passage is to be interpreted dualistically. In these Scriptures, you will see a mix of typological, historical events, and their ultimate prophetic fulfillment reserved for the last days.

Historically speaking, this last attempt by Antiochus IV fell short because of the intervention of Rome. They did this by sending ships from Cyprus to deliver an ultimatum from the Senate to Antiochus IV to cease and desist his aggression against Egypt. It is said that a Roman officer, Gaius Popilius Laenas, was chosen and sent by the Senate of Rome because he was a friend of Antiochus IV. They had both been groomed in the royal courts of Rome from their childhood to serve the empire in positions of strategic importance. When Antiochus IV received the senate's decree, he asked for time to consider it. It is said that the Roman officer then drew a circle in the sand around Antiochus IV and told him that he expected his decision before he stepped out of that circle. Antiochus, knowing full well the Roman ways and military power, totally understood the gravity of his choice. He relented, broke off his attack on Egypt, and retreated back to his own country, enraged because of his unfulfilled ambitions. He vented that rage on Israel, whose traditions he had been patiently undermining by a systematic persuasion of the people to indulge themselves in a Hellenistic way of life (Grecian social influence). He showed regard for and favored those who were forsaking God's holy covenant to serve this hedonistic lifestyle (decadent lifestyle of satisfying carnal pleasures). Through flattery and deceit, he subverted many of God's people and their spiritual leaders to give their allegiance to him and his gods. He divided the house of God one against the other and persecuted without mercy those who remained faithful to God and His ways. He defiled the temple, took away the daily sacrifices, and made unlawful all public worship of God. He burned any written copies of the law that were found, killing those who possessed them. He forbad circumcision and hung the sons who were circumcised around the necks of their mothers before executing the parents. Many of those who were persecuted for these and other offenses were made known to this corrupt government through the betrayal of their own family members. However, there was a remnant that would not bow their knees to him and his evil ways, choosing instead to risk martyrdom that they might instruct many in the ways of God. This is recorded in history as the Maccabean revolt lasting seven years from 167 to 160 BC.

Though Antiochus did many abominable things and caused many desolations in Israel, the "abomination of desolation" spoken of by Daniel and quoted by Jesus in Matthew chapter twenty-four is not a historical event but a prophetic event that is yet to happen. Jesus declares that this prophecy will occur in the last days as a part of the greatest tribulation that has ever been or ever will be on this earth. Antiochus' offering of the pig on the brazen altar of the man-made temple is only typological of the abomination of desolation that Jesus was referring to near the end of this age. For more explanation, please see "The Abomination of Desolation," which is in chapter six of my previous book, *The Terminal Generation*.

You will notice the phrase, "at the appointed time," is used on three occasions in Daniel, chapter eleven. I remind you of what was shared in the previous chapter about this phrase. The phrase, "At the appointed time" is 'mow ed' in the Hebrew language. It means an appointed time/season, a sacred/set feast or festival, an appointed sign or signal of a prophetic event that is yet to come. This phrase is used by God in Daniel to reference a transition from a historical to an eschatological fulfillment of the dualistic prophecy.

I believe that most of what Antiochus IV did during his reign was typological of an ultimate prophetic fulfillment of Daniel's visions. What was limited to the holy land and the Israelites in Antiochus' day will become a universal reality. The Antichrist will prosecute and persecute God's people of every nation, kindred, and tongue during the great tribulation of the saints. They will be tested and suffer many things for Jesus' namesake. Revelation 7:14 testifies of these saying, "These are the ones who come out of the great tribulation, and washed their robes and made them white in the blood of the Lamb." As with Antiochus IV, so it will be with the Antichrist. The ultimate prophetic fulfillment will follow the pattern of the earlier typological. The Antichrist will also defile the temple, which today is the church made up of living stones. He will take away the daily sacrifices and make unlawful all public expressions of the worship of God. He will not be deterred by any other but will do according to his own will and pleasure. He will exalt himself above all, even above the God of all gods, the King of all kings, and the Lord of all lords. He will regard and honor a powerful god his fathers did not intimately know. Revelation chapters twelve and thirteen identify this god who will give him his power and authority as being the great red dragon, who is none other than Satan. God will allow him to reign and persecute the saints of the Most High God for three and a half years – Daniel 7:25. I encourage you to read Revelation 13:1-18 at this time.

This passage goes on to say that at the time of the end, the king of the South will attack the king of the North. The king of the North, like a whirlwind, will finally overwhelm and destroy Egypt and overthrow many other countries. He will plant his palace between the seas and the glorious holy mountain (Mt. Zion) in Israel. The passage below concludes with the sudden demise and destruction of the Antichrist, and no one will be able to deliver him from his fate. John prophesies in Revelation 19:20 that the Beast/Antichrist and the false prophet will be captured and cast alive into the lake of fire burning with brimstone.

I have included the passage below as a reference to aid you in considering the views I have shared above. Let me be quick to say that I in no way want to come across as being dogmatic in my beliefs. They are merely the machinations of what I see now as I look through the dark glass of Daniel's prophecies. I reserve the right to change my views at a moment's notice as God sheds His light on His Word. I feel somewhat like the blind man Jesus healed, who was able to see men walking as trees. Eventually, the Lord caused him to see clearly what once was blurry in the process of curing him of his blindness. I too, like the blind man, am in God's process whereby He is causing me to see more clearly through His unsealing of what has been mystically obscured for thousands of years.

> 29"At the appointed time he shall return and go toward
> the south, but it shall not be like the former or the latter.
> 30For ships from Cyprus shall come against him; there-
> fore, he shall be grieved, and return in rage against the
> holy covenant, and do damage. "So he shall return and
> show regard for those who forsake the holy covenant.

[31]And forces shall be mustered by him, and they shall
defile the sanctuary fortress; then they shall take away
the daily sacrifices, and place there the abomination of
desolation. [32]Those who do wickedly against the covenant he shall corrupt with flattery, but the people who
know their God shall be strong, and carry out great
exploits. [33]And those of the people who understand
shall instruct many; yet for many days they shall fall by
sword and flame, by captivity and plundering. [34]Now
when they fall, they shall be aided with a little help; but
many shall join with them by intrigue. [35]And some of
those of understanding shall fall, to refine them, purify
them, and make them white, until the time of the end;
because it is still for the appointed time. [36]"Then the
king shall do according to his own will: he shall exalt
and magnify himself above every god, shall speak blas-
phemies against the God of gods, and shall prosper till
the wrath has been accomplished; for what has been
determined shall be done. [37]He shall regard neither the
God of his fathers nor the desire of women, nor regard
any god; for he shall exalt himself above them all. [38]But
in their place he shall honor a god of fortresses; and
a god which his fathers did not know he shall honor
with gold and silver, with precious stones and pleasant
things. [39]Thus he shall act against the strongest fortresses with a foreign god, which he shall acknowledge,
and advance its glory; and he shall cause them to rule
over many, and divide the land for gain. [40]"At the time of
the end the king of the South shall attack him; and the
king of the North shall come against him like a whirlwind, with chariots, horsemen, and with many ships;

> and he shall enter the countries, overwhelm them, and pass through. 41He shall also enter the Glorious Land, and many countries shall be overthrown; but these shall escape from his hand: Edom, Moab, and the prominent people of Ammon. 42He shall stretch out his hand against the countries, and the land of Egypt shall not escape. 43He shall have power over the treasures of gold and silver, and over all the precious things of Egypt; also the Libyans and Ethiopians shall follow at his heels. 44But news from the east and the north shall trouble him; therefore he shall go out with great fury to destroy and annihilate many. 45And he shall plant the tents of his palace between the seas and the glorious holy mountain, yet he shall come to his end, and no one will help him.
>
> —Daniel 11:29-45

Having read this lengthy portion of Scripture, it is evident a dualistic interpretation was intended by God. One can see the historical/typological fulfillment as well as the ultimate prophetic fulfillment that is yet to happen.

I want to encourage you to seek the Lord for the unveiling of what was hidden and sealed. I believe the time of the end is near, and the appointed time of Daniel's unsealing is upon us.

CHAPTER 5

REVELATIONS IN DANIEL 12

Introduction

Chapter twelve of Daniel is a continuation of the revelation Daniel received in the previous chapter during the first year of the reign of King Darius. Chapter eleven's narrative concludes with an elaboration of the rise and fall of the Antichrist. Let's begin to investigate in Daniel, chapter twelve, what else God wants to reveal about this crucial time and its related events.

Daniel, Chapter Twelve

The first verse seamlessly expands on the very same time frame by supplying additional information relative to that period. It adds the fact that at that very same time, Michael, the great prince who watches over God's people, shall stand up. I believe this event has more considerable eschatological significance than mere chit-chat offered as a greeting before a serious discussion.

> [1]"At that time Michael shall stand up, the great prince who stands watch over the sons of your people; and there shall be a time of trouble, such as never was since there was a nation, even to that time. And at that time your people shall be delivered, every one who is found written in the book. —Daniel 12:1

Notice Daniel indicated that during the time of the Antichrist there shall also be a time of trouble such as never was, since there was a nation even up to the start of that trouble. This is a direct reference to the great tribulation as depicted by Jesus in His teaching on the Mount of Olives in Matthew 24:21-22.

> [21]For then there will be great tribulation, such as has not been since the beginning of the world until this time, no, nor ever shall be. [22]And unless those days were shortened, no flesh would be saved; but for the elect's sake, those days will be shortened. —Matthew 24:21-22

What about the reference to Michael standing up at that time? Is that significant? I believe it is another confirmation concerning the tribulation period and other prophetic events that surround its beginning. Revelation twelve talks about the woman fleeing into the wilderness after the firstfruits manchild is caught up to the throne of God. The woman, who is the church or the Israel of God, will be tribulated by the great red dragon for 1260 days (3½ years) after the war in heaven is concluded. For more details on Revelation chapter twelve, I encourage you to read chapters thirteen and fourteen of the prequel, *The Terminal Generation.* I devote two entire chapters on the characters and events of that Scripture passage. Let's look at a portion of that passage of Scripture to provide a further understanding of what Daniel was saying.

> 5She bore a male Child who was to rule all nations with
> a rod of iron. And her Child was caught up to God and
> His throne. 6Then the woman fled into the wilderness,
> where she has a place prepared by God, that they
> should feed her there one thousand two hundred and
> sixty days. 7And war broke out in heaven: Michael and
> his angels fought with the dragon; and the dragon and
> his angels fought, 8but they did not prevail, nor was a
> place found for them in heaven any longer. 9So the great
> dragon was cast out, that serpent of old called the Devil
> and Satan, who deceives the whole world; he was cast
> to the earth, and his angels were cast out with him.
>
> —Revelation 12:5-9

Notice in verse 7 that a war broke out in heaven between Michael and his angels and Satan and his angels. This passage goes on to say that Satan and his angels lost the battle and were permanently cast out of heaven and restricted to the earthly realm only. Reading further, we learn that Satan is very angry with these new arrangements and vents his fury on God's people. The conclusion of the war in heaven begins the great tribulation. Daniel's reference to Michael standing up is speaking to the beginning of a time of trouble for God's people. He offers consolation, however, by declaring that all of God's people who are found written in the book of life shall be delivered.

Daniel, chapter twelve, verse two, can be a little confusing as it seems to infer that there will be one general resurrection and judgment where both the righteous and the wicked will be judged at the same time. We have to be careful when developing a doctrinal position. We form it by gleaning from all the Scriptures that talk about the subject. Remember, Scripture never contradicts itself. I want to share again a divine principle I related in *The Terminal Generation*. Several years ago, God spoke to me in a time of devotion. It was about a hermeneutic (an approach to interpreting Scripture) that I should be careful to implement when it comes to forming and holding a doctrinal position. He said, "When your position satisfies one Scripture and violates another, you must believe Me to enlighten you to a position that satisfies both." With that in mind, let us take a look at verse two.

> 2And many of those who sleep in the dust of the earth shall awake, some to everlasting life, some to shame and everlasting contempt. —Daniel 12:2

The one general resurrection and judgment interpretation of verse two would violate several other Scriptures that deal with the resurrection of the dead and eternal judgment. Several Scriptures clearly teach that there are two resurrections followed by two judgments. These would be in contradiction to and violate the Daniel passage if verse two really was speaking of one general resurrection. Let's look at the biblical verses that speak of two resurrections and then see how to reconcile them with Daniel 12:2.

> 4And I saw thrones, and they sat on them, and judgment was committed to them. Then I saw the souls of those who had been beheaded for their witness to Jesus and for the word of God, who had not worshiped the beast or his image and had not received his mark on their foreheads or on their hands. And they lived and
> reigned with Christ for a thousand years. 5But the rest
> of the dead did not live again until the thousand years
> were finished. This is the first resurrection. 6Blessed and
> holy is he who has part in the first resurrection. Over such the second death has no power, but they shall be priests of God and of Christ and shall reign with Him a thousand years. —Revelation 20:4-6

Notice that this passage of Scripture teaches two resurrections separated by a thousand years. All the dead who are raised before the millennial kingdom are a part of the first resurrection and the second death has no power over them. Paul speaks of this same resurrection in more detail in 1 Thessalonians chapter four where he says that at the rapture the dead in Christ will rise first and then we who are alive and remain shall be caught up together with them in the clouds to meet and forever be with the Lord. These shall rule and reign with Christ for a thousand years (millennial kingdom). The only graves that will not be opened at this time are of those who died as unbelievers. Reading verses 11-15 of this same chapter, you will notice that the unopened graves will be opened at the end of the millennial kingdom and those who are raised shall stand before God at the Great White Throne Judgment.

This Scripture from Luke confirms two resurrections.

> [14]And you will be blessed because they cannot repay you; for you shall be repaid at the resurrection of the just."
> —Luke 14:14

This Scripture says that believers will be rewarded for their kindness at the resurrection of the just. This infers that there will be a resurrection of the unjust that is different. They are not a part of one resurrection but are, in fact, two separate resurrections. When comparing this passage with the previous one we shared, we also know that they occur at different times.

Also, in the following passage from John, we see once again that there are two distinct resurrections – the resurrection of life and the resurrection of condemnation. Though this Scripture speaks of two resurrections, it does not speak to the timing of such. However, we know that this verse cannot be in violation of the Revelation chapter twenty passage.

> [28] Do not marvel at this; for the hour is coming in which all who are in the graves will hear His voice 29 and come forth—those who have done good, to the resurrection of life, and those who have done evil, to the resurrection of condemnation.
> —John 5:28-29

Considering the above Scriptures, how does one reconcile them to be congruent with verse two of Daniel twelve?

Notice that verse says that many who sleep in the dust of the earth shall awake; it didn't say all, which would indicate one general raising of the dead. Once again, I reiterate that the verse in Daniel cannot violate any other Scripture concerning the first and second resurrections and/or their timing.

After having talked about the resurrections in verse two, Daniel transitions back to the saints during the great tribulation. Paul states that believers enter the kingdom through the process of much tribulation. God's purpose for trials has always been to cleanse, purify, and mature His saints to reflect His nature and draw many to His glorious light. In verse three, Daniel declares that those tribulated will shine like the brightness of the firmament and turn many to righteousness.

> 3Those who are wise shall shine like the brightness of the firmament, and those who turn many to righteousness like the stars forever and ever. —Daniel 12:3

At this juncture, Daniel is commanded by God to shut up the words and seal the book until the time of the end.

> 4"But you, Daniel, shut up the words, and seal the book until the time of the end; many shall run to and fro, and knowledge shall increase." —Daniel 12:4

God describes this time of the end as being a time when many would run to and fro, and knowledge shall increase. First of all, what does God mean by the phrase, "Many shall run to and fro?" Until the last century, most of mankind never traveled far from where they were born and raised. Today, however, in the advent of modern transportation, people are going around the globe daily. Can there be any doubt that this present generation is fulfilling this end-time prophetic verse? Secondly, what does God mean by the phrase, "Knowledge shall increase?" At no other time in recorded history do we see such an exponential increase in knowledge as we have seen in this last century. Not only the quantity of knowledge which has been attained but also the quantum speed with which it is being reached is unprecedented. Even today, all we have to do is to speak to our cell phone to have access to all the treasures of knowledge that has been accumulated throughout the annals of time.

It is interesting to note that immediately after God instructed Daniel to shut up and seal the book until the time of the end, He caused Daniel to see a vision. From this vision, God continued to reveal more about the very subject He charged Daniel to seal.

> 5Then I, Daniel, looked; and there stood two others, one on this riverbank and the other on that riverbank. 6And one said to the man clothed in linen, who was above the waters of the river, "How long shall the fulfillment of these wonders be?" 7Then I heard the man clothed in linen, who was above the waters of the river, when he held up his right hand and his left hand to heaven and swore by Him who lives forever, that it shall be for a time, times, and half a time; and when the power of the holy people has been completely shattered, all these things shall be finished. —Daniel 12:5-7

In this vision, Daniel saw two heavenly beings on opposite sides of a riverbank, with one asking a question of the man dressed in linen, who was above the river waters. Being clothed in white linen was indicative of the apparel worn by those who were priests. Could the one in white linens be our High Priest, the pre-incarnate Christ? The question he posed was about how long it will take for the wonders previously being discussed to reach their fulfillment. His answer was that it shall be for a time, times, and half a time, which is three and a half years.

If we are to understand the question, it is essential that we know what this time-period is referring to. The context of the previous verses is about the tribulation period as well as the events that surround it. One of the most important considerations about the great tribulation is that the saints will be vulnerable to the persecution by the Antichrist until that time is over. The question would then read, "How long will the tribulation period be to reach its fulfillment?" Numerous Scriptures would confirm the answer given in verse seven. These Scriptures use different descriptors such as "time, times, and half a time, forty-two months, or 1260 days," but they all mean the same thing. This is an important truth to establish since many Christians have been taught the tribulation period is seven years long, a fact that cannot be confirmed by Scripture.

After clearly seeing the vision and hearing the question with its answer, Daniel's response was that, even though he saw and heard, he did not understand. This prompted him to ask the Lord how all these things will end. Once again, the

Lord told Daniel to go his way, for these things are closed up and sealed until the time of the end. And then, right on the heels of God telling Daniel to stop pressing Him for more understanding of these matters, He gave Daniel a little more information. God said to him that many shall be purified, made white, and refined during this time, while at the same time the wicked shall do wickedly. He continued by saying that in the end the wicked will not understand, but the wise will understand, the very things of which Daniel lacked understanding. They would understand what was hidden to Daniel because they would be alive at the time of the unsealing of that which was sealed.

> 8Although I heard, I did not understand. Then I said, "My lord, what shall be the end of these things?" 9And he said, "Go your way, Daniel, for the words are closed up and sealed till the time of the end. 10Many shall be purified, made white, and refined, but the wicked shall do wickedly; and none of the wicked shall understand, but the wise shall understand. —Daniel 12:8-10

In the next two verses, the Lord continued giving even more information about the time period following the great tribulation.

> 11"And from the time that the daily sacrifice is taken away, and the abomination of desolation is set up, there shall be one thousand two hundred and ninety days. 12Blessed is he who waits, and comes to the one thousand three hundred and thirty-five days.
>
> —Daniel 12:11-12

It is during the tribulation that the saints will be purified, made white, and refined. It is during the tribulation that the daily sacrifice will be taken away, and the abomination of desolation will be set up. He is telling Daniel that, from the time of the tribulation, there will be a 1290-day time period. What time period is being spoken of here? Revelation, chapter six and seven speak of it as the great day of God's wrath. The announcement of the impending wrath of God is recorded in the sixth seal. The implementation of this judgment is graphically described in the seventh seal, which is made up of seven trumpets. Whereas the great tribulation has to do with the persecution of the saints, this time period has to do with the judgment of the wicked.

Now, I would like to elaborate on the three time periods Daniel speaks about concerning the last seven years of this age. Again, before doing so, let me reiterate that what I am about to share is not to be misconstrued as being dogmatic. It is merely what I feel the Lord has spoken to me as I have sought Him on these matters. I fully understand that now we hear and know in part. However, I offer what I believe the Lord has shown me for your consideration.

And now let us take a closer look at the three time periods referenced by Daniel. These commence with the great tribulation and conclude before the start of the millennial kingdom. It is my belief these define time spans that pertain to the great tribulation, the great day of God's wrath, and the interval between the rapture and the second coming.

Let's consider the great tribulation first. Daniel defines its span as being a time, times, and half a time, which is three and a half years. John, the revelator, describes this same event as being forty-two months, or 1260 days, which are also three and a half years. This brings us to the middle of the week or the halfway point of the last seven years of this age.

Now let us consider the great day of God's wrath, also known as the "Day of the Lord." I personally believe the "1290" time period refers to the duration of this future prophetic event. Let me share with you why I believe this. The great day of God's wrath is described by the seven trumpets/bowls that make up the seventh seal. The trumpets are broken up into two groups. The first four are poured out as judgments on the environment in which man lives. The last three are described as the three woes that follow the first four. Each woe is increasingly more severe than what preceded it. When reading about the two witnesses of Revelation eleven, it is unmistakable that, though their ministry lasted 1260 days, the period during which they ministered was within the 1290 days. You can read more about the two witnesses in chapter twenty-five of *The Terminal Generation*. At the conclusion of their ministry, they were killed and left unburied in the streets for 3½ days. Then God raised them from the dead, and they ascended into heaven – see Revelation 11.

> [11]Now after the three-and-a-half days, the breath of life from God entered them, and they stood on their feet, and great fear fell on those who saw them. [12]And they heard a loud voice from heaven saying to them, "Come up here." And they ascended to heaven in a cloud, and

> their enemies saw them. [13]In the same hour, there was a great earthquake, and a tenth of the city fell. In the earthquake, seven thousand people were killed, and the rest were afraid and gave glory to the God of heaven. [14]The second woe is past. Behold, the third woe is coming quickly. —Revelation 11:11-14

After their ascension, verse fourteen states that the second woe is past and the third woe is coming quickly. This means that the "Day of the Lord" is 1260 days long plus whatever time it takes to pour out the seventh or last trumpet. Interestingly, the beginning of the feast of trumpets is referred to in Jewish tradition as the day or hour that no man knows. This feast officially begins when the priest sights the new moon in the month of Tishri. However, this varied from year to year, and they often had to watch for a couple of days before sighting the new moon. They truly never knew by counting the days from the last new moon. God sovereignly dictated the timing as part of His process to keep the lunar and solar calendars in sync. Because of this they never knew the day or the hour of the beginning of the only feast (feast of trumpets) that began on the first day of a month. The rapture will take place during this fall feast at the seventh or last trump. I believe in the year that the rapture happens, the new moon will not be sighted at the close of the twelfth month (Adar) to establish the first day of the first month (Nissan) of the new year. When that happened periodically, the High Priest was instructed to add another thirty days (Adar II) to the current year before beginning the new year on Nissan 1. In the year prior to the rapture taking place,

I genuinely believe this will be the case. It will result in thirty days being added that year. This will result in the last half of the final week of this age being thirty days longer than the first half. We know that the first half of the last week, which constitutes the great tribulation, will be 1260 days. Adding thirty days to the last year of this age would cause the duration of the last half of the final week to total 1290 days.

Finally, let's consider the interval between the rapture and the second coming (the literal return of Jesus to the earth), which are definitely not the same event. Remember, after the rapture the saints of God will take part in the judgment seat of Christ, the wedding & the marriage supper of the Lamb, and the second coming of Jesus with His army. I personally believe that the 1335-day time period refers to the interval between the end of the great tribulation and the second coming of Christ (see Appendix A). Notice that the rapture takes place at the beginning of the seventh trump, which is 1290 days after the conclusion of the great tribulation. Forty-five days after the rapture, which totals 1335, the second coming takes place. If I am correct, the forty-five days marks the time period on earth to complete the seventh trumpet while at the same time the raptured saints are experiencing the judgment of the righteous, the wedding, and the marriage feast.

I know that many scholars may not agree with my conclusion, but one thing is sure; God will make it clear at the end of this age when He unseals that which Daniel was commanded to seal.

> 3"But you, go your way till the end; for you shall rest, and will arise to your inheritance at the end of the days."
> —Daniel 12:13

God concludes by telling Daniel that the revelation session is over and that he would die but be raised to participate in his inheritance at the very time period about which Daniel had been prophesying.

SECTION 2

The Revelations in Daniel

(The Seventieth Week of Daniel)

CHAPTER 6

Introduction ~ What Is It?

Introduction to the Study

The seventieth week of Daniel is a description of a biblical prophecy found in Daniel 9:24-27. This was a prophetic word concerning the nation of Israel and the city of Jerusalem given to the Jews while they were in captivity in Babylon. In contrast to many of her other prophecies, which are repeated in multiple places in the Scriptures, there is no other prophetic mention of this period or event. An example of an often-mentioned prophetic promise given to Israel is the coming of Israel's Messiah. This promise is found in numerous biblical passages. However, there is only one biblical reference to the seventy weeks of Daniel. I have included below the passage we will be studying in Section 2.

> [24]"Seventy weeks are determined for your people and for your holy city, to finish the transgression, to make an

> end of sins, to make reconciliation for iniquity, to bring in everlasting righteousness, to seal up vision and prophecy, and to anoint the Most Holy. [25]"Know therefore and understand, that from the going forth of the command to restore and build Jerusalem until Messiah the Prince, there shall be seven weeks and sixty-two weeks; the street shall be built again, and the wall, even in troublesome times. [26]"And after the sixty-two weeks Messiah shall be cut off, but not for Himself, and the people of the prince who is to come shall destroy the city and the sanctuary. The end of it shall be with a flood, and till the end of the war, desolations are determined. [27]Then he shall confirm a covenant with many for one week, but in the middle of the week, He shall bring an end to sacrifice and offering. And on the wing of abominations shall be one who makes desolate, even until the consummation, which is determined, is poured out on the desolate. —Daniel 9:24-27

This prophecy was given to Daniel by the angel Gabriel. As in their previous meeting, Gabriel announced that he was sent by God to Daniel to give him skill and understanding concerning end times and what the future would hold for Israel.

Many doctrines concerning eschatology for Israel and the Church have been built and based on this one short passage of Scripture. I must say at this point that a good portion of this doctrine has been formulated using an inferior hermeneutical approach. I will discuss this subject in greater detail in addressing the questions I raise below.

CHAPTER 6: INTRODUCTION – WHAT IS IT?

The following are pertinent questions that need to be scrutinized from the Scriptures rather than blindly receiving commonly orthodox teachings by popular ministries. Does the above passage speak of a seven-year peace treaty with Israel at the end of this age? Does it speak of the Great Tribulation Period and the rebuilding of a temple in Jerusalem? Does it speak of a two-thousand-year gap between the 69th and 70th weeks of Daniel? Is it possible that there are both typological and ultimate prophetic fulfillments of this Scripture?

In the following pages, I will endeavor to answer these as well as other questions concerning this prophecy. I also want to share its relevance to other eschatological prophecies and its place in God's prophetic timeline. It is helpful to understand that this passage can be divided into three: 1) Daniel 9:24 contains a "general" statement of what would occur in the specified seventy-week time period; 2) Daniel 9:25-26 speaks of how that would unfold and be accomplished. In this statement, the whole time period of the seventy weeks is broken up into three smaller portions of seven weeks, sixty-two weeks, and one week, with each designating some specific time period; 3) Daniel 9:27 gives greater specificity and additional detail to the events occurring during the seventieth week of Daniel as spoken of in verse 26. I personally believe that this week is a shadow of a coming week that will take place long after the conclusion of the seventy weeks. According to Paul, Israel's history was to serve as a shadow picture of what the church should expect in her future.

> 11Now all these things happened to them as examples, and they were written for our admonition, upon whom the ends of the ages have come. —1 Corinthians 10:11

The last week of this age will be patterned after the seventieth (last) week of Daniel, which is a typological prophetic fulfillment concerning Israel and Jerusalem. I believe this last week will be the ultimate prophetic fulfillment purposed for the Church, Israel, and Jerusalem at the end of this age. It is important to note that the last seven years of this age will be subdivided into two 3½-year periods. We will discuss this in greater detail later.

Introduction of the Prophecy

The introduction of this prophecy begins with a declaration from Gabriel that God has predetermined seventy weeks that will have significant relevance to the future of the nation of Israel and the holy city, Jerusalem. The Hebrew word for *determined* in verse 24 means "to be decreed or marked out." Gabriel's announcement was to serve as an awakening to the nation that God had marked out a specific period of time in this age for a particular purpose. It was a call to be watchful for particular events God prophesied would happen in both their near and distant future. This nation had been lulled asleep by almost seventy years of captivity in Babylon. The Israelites knew they were under the judgment of God for their past failures. They had become accustomed to their lot in life, and most had little expectation or hope of that changing in their lifetime. Most had forgotten or never knew of the prophecies of Jeremiah warning them of their immediate demise. The prophet told Israel's leaders that judgment would come if they did not turn back to and honor God and His ways. He was considered to be a doomsday prophet by most. While most of the other prophets were prophesying good things to the nation before their captivity, Jeremiah's message was anything but good. He was considered dangerous to the morale of the country and was eventually imprisoned for his negativity.

Even Daniel was reminded of and understood the word of the Lord for his people, as he read the prophecy of Jeremiah while in captivity in the palace of Shushan. Shushan was the capital of the empire of the Medes and Persians who defeated King Belshazzar of Babylon. Daniel saw his future in a vision as being in another palace in a different city even before Babylon's fall. This vision became a reality after Babylon fell to King Darius of the Medes and King Cyrus of the Persians. Darius ruled first before Cyrus. In the first year of his reign, Daniel was reading the written prophecies of Jeremiah and was given an understanding that the time of Israel's and Jerusalem's judgment would be seventy years.

> [2]in the first year of his reign I, Daniel, understood by the books the number of the years specified by the word of the Lord through Jeremiah the prophet, that He would accomplish seventy years in the desolations of Jerusalem.
> —Daniel 9:2

I believe Daniel was reading the words of Jeremiah, as recorded in Jeremiah, chapters 25 and 29.

> [11]And this whole land shall be a desolation and an astonishment, and these nations shall serve the king of Babylon seventy years. [12]'Then it will come to pass, when seventy years are completed, that I will punish the king of Babylon and that nation, the land of the Chaldeans, for their iniquity,' says the LORD; 'and I will make it a perpetual desolation. —Jeremiah 25:11-12

> [10]For thus says the Lord: After seventy years are completed at Babylon, I will visit you and perform My good word toward you, and cause you to return to this place. [11]For I know the thoughts that I think toward you, says the Lord, thoughts of peace and not of evil, to give you a future and a hope. —Jeremiah 29:10-11

Once he understood, he began to seek the Lord for direction for his people with prayer and fasting. He confessed the sins of himself and God's people. He acknowledged that they had not hearkened to the prophets God sent to warn them and declared Israel's failure to keep the laws and ordinances of God as the reason for the evil judgments that had befallen them. He sought God to once again show His mercy, as He had done in delivering Israel out of Egypt, and that the Lord would restore His sanctuary that was made desolate.

As Daniel was asking for forgiveness for himself and his people, Gabriel appeared and touched him about the time of the evening oblation. As in his previous visitation, Gabriel repeated that he was sent by God to give Daniel skill and understanding in things which would happen in Israel's future. He told Daniel that from the very time he began to offer up his prayers of supplication with fasting, God had commanded him to come to help Daniel understand, because he was much loved by God.

CHAPTER 7

Six Purposes

The Six Purposes

Daniel was told that seventy weeks were determined on Israel and the holy city of Jerusalem. He was made to know that God decided that six things would be accomplished concerning Israel and Jerusalem during the time of these seventy weeks. These six things are recorded in Daniel 9:24.

> [24]"Seventy weeks are determined For your people and for your holy city, To finish the transgression, To make an end of sins, To make reconciliation for iniquity, To bring in everlasting righteousness, To seal up vision and prophecy, And to anoint the Most Holy. —Daniel 9:24

It is clear from this Scripture that all six of these things transpire during the seventy weeks prophesied by Daniel. None of them are accomplished outside of these 490 years. Now let's take a look at and describe what these six things are which were to be fulfilled within 490 years from a specified date.

Finish the Transgression

What did God mean by the phrase, "To finish the transgression"? The Hebrew word *pesha* means transgression, rebellion, trespass, or sin. "To finish" means to complete the course or finish something that has begun. Let's look at Israel's history to see if we can gain some insights as to what God might be referring to in this passage. Several things in Israel's past strike me as significant transgressions or acts of rebellion against God's clearly stated will.

The first instance I want to mention has to do with God's purpose and destiny for His chosen people, Israel. Through Moses, God offered to make Israel a people of His own with the prestigious position of being a royal priesthood representing the kingdom of God to this earth. With this position came the right and ability to stand in the presence of God. Priests were those who had access to God with the responsibility to minister to, and on behalf of, those who did not have access to the presence of God. God desired to fill this earth with the abundant life of His glorious kingdom using Israel as priests to represent Him. The children of Israel initially agreed to be those priests. God gave them two days to cleanse and make themselves ready to stand as priests in His presence. When that day finally arrived, His presence and His voice were so terrifying that His chosen people did not want to stand in His presence and hear His voice directly again. They said they would rather have Moses listen to God and then report to them what He said. Since they rejected the priesthood, God had to find someone else to fulfill this destiny. I personally believe this act of rebellion was the beginning of Israel's transgression from God's intended purpose for them. This choice sealed their fate from which they would never recover even to the end of this age. When the transgression of Israel had finished its course, God turned to the Church and offered the priesthood to her. The fact that the choice Israel made is still affecting them to this day can be seen in Hebrews 12:18-25, which records the story just shared above. Verse 25 of this passage makes it very clear that if they did not escape the judgment of God for refusing to hear His voice, who spoke to them on this earth, then neither will the Church escape if they, like Israel, refuse to listen to the voice of God that speaks from heaven.

> 25See that you do not refuse Him who speaks. For if they did not escape who refused Him who spoke on earth, much more shall we not escape if we turn away from Him who speaks from heaven —Hebrews 12:25

As members of the church of Jesus Christ, let us not make the same mistake of not appearing before the Lord inside the Holy Place (Mountain) to stand in His presence and hear His voice.

Another instance I would like to cite concerning the ongoing transgression of Israel deals with her failure to obey the command to make every seventh year a sabbath year, which was to be a year of rest for the people, the land, and the economy. It is referred to in the Bible as the year of the Shemitah. The reason God had allowed the Israelites to be taken captive by the Babylonians was that Israel transgressed against the Lord by not observing the Shemitah year. God sentenced them to seventy years of captivity based on the number of Shemitahs they failed to keep. Look at Leviticus 26:32-35:

> [32]I will bring the land to desolation, and your enemies who dwell in it shall be astonished at it. [33]I will scatter you among the nations and draw out a sword after you; your land shall be desolate and your cities waste. [34]Then the land shall enjoy its sabbaths as long as it lies desolate and you are in your enemies' land; then the land shall rest and enjoy its sabbaths. [35]As long as it lies desolate it shall rest—for the time it did not rest on your sabbaths when you dwelt in it.
>
> —Leviticus 26:32-35

The math is fascinating. If Israel skipped seventy Shemitahs and there was a Shemitah every seven years, then Israel's transgression in this instance spanned 490 years before their being scattered into captivity. At the end of the seventy years of Babylonian captivity, Daniel received a prophecy concerning Israel's future. This prophecy stated that there would be another span of 490 years (seventy weeks) in which the cup of their transgression would reach its fullness (Daniel 9:24). After these 490 years, the transgression of Israel would reach its climatic end of the longsuffering of God with the destruction of Jerusalem in 70 AD. Jesus prophesied of this in Luke 19.

> [41]Now as He drew near, He saw the city and wept over it, [42]saying, "If you had known, even you, especially in this

> your day, the things that make for your peace! But now they are hidden from your eyes. [43]For days will come upon you when your enemies will build an embankment around you, surround you and close you in on every side, [44]and level you, and your children within you, to the ground; and they will not leave in you one stone upon another, because you did not know the time of your visitation."
>
> —Luke 19:41-44

History records the span of this captivity as beginning in 70 AD and ending in 1948 for the nation and 1967 for Jerusalem, which is almost 2,000 years.

Jesus also spoke of this judgment in His eschatological teaching in Luke 21:24. This is a vivid description of what happens when the transgression is finished after the seventieth week of Daniel.

> [24]And they will fall by the edge of the sword, and be led away captive into all nations. And Jerusalem will be trampled by Gentiles until the times of the Gentiles are fulfilled.
>
> —Luke 21:24

Another interesting note about 490 years can be seen in Matthew 18. Here Peter was asking the Lord how many times one should forgive a brother that sins against him.

> [21]Then came Peter to him, and said, Lord, how oft shall my brother sin against me, and I forgive him? till seven times? [22]Jesus saith unto him, I say not unto thee, Until seven times: but, Until seventy times seven.
>
> —Matthew 18:21-22

God was holding His children to the same standard concerning forgiveness that He had Himself observed on these two occasions stated above. Some have interpreted this passage to mean that forgiveness is to have no boundaries or limitations. God's dealings with His people and even with other nations shows clearly that the cup of God's indignation can be filled to overflowing. There are boundaries and limitations to this cup. However, we also see that after the appropriate judgment was served by the transgressors, God again forgave them and started afresh the relationship once held by the two parties previously.

Make an End of Sins

What did God mean by the phrase, "To make an end of sins?" Sin is the simple part of understanding this phrase, so let's deal with that first. The Hebrew word for sin here is *chattaath*, which comes from the root word, *chata*. This word means to sin, miss, or miss the mark. This is an archery term used by judges in an archery contest. When an archer shot at a target, and it missed right, left, short, or above the target, the judge would cry aloud, "Sin." Therefore, we can conclude that sin is merely missing the mark (the bullseye) on the target, which is the goal and standard of God. This gives new meaning to the verse that all have sinned and fallen short of the glory of God. As in archery, the goal of God is that we not walk left or right of His ways – see Joshua 1:7. Nor are we to stop short of or go beyond His ways – see Romans 3:23 and 1 Corinthians 4:6. The only way to not hear God, the Judge, cry out, "Sin," is that we stay in the center of God's will, as evidenced by hitting the bullseye. I think we all would rather hear the judge cry out "bullseye" rather than "sin."

Now let's deal with the more difficult part of the above phrase. Two Hebrew words are used in the phrase "to make an end." The first word is *Tamam*, which primarily means, "to complete or finish." The second word is *Chatham*, which primarily means "to seal up, lock up, or hide from view." The phrase could then be read as "to seal up, lock up, remove from God's sight," or even, "to take away sin." Was John the Baptist speaking of this very thing in John 1:39 when he said, "Behold the Lamb of God, which taketh away the sin of the world?" When that Lamb was slain there was no longer a need for sacrifices and oblations. How could this change the meaning of how one might interpret the second in this list of six things that would be accomplished during the seventy weeks of Daniel?

Consider for a moment what effect sin has on God's people. I would like to first pose a question to you, the reader. If I were to ask you the question, "What was the purpose or end goal of Jesus' suffering and dying for us," what would your answer be? Most to whom I have asked this question quickly answer, "Christ suffered and died for my sins." You may or may not have answered the same. To those who did, I would like to suggest that your answer was a means to His objective, but it was not His purpose or end goal. I personally believe His end goal is clearly stated in 1 Peter 3:18.

> 18For Christ also suffered once for sins, the just for the unjust, that He might bring us to God, being put to

death in the flesh but made alive by the Spirit.

—1 Peter 3:18

Notice that the goal for Christ's suffering and dying was to bring us back to God. Isaiah 59:2 says that it is our iniquities and sins that have separated us from our God and hidden His face from us. Therefore, suffering and dying for our sins was a means to the end of bringing us back from being separated from God. In the old covenant dispensation, the sins of God's people were atoned for and covered for one year. This necessitated an annual blood sacrifice to deal with the sins and iniquities that would otherwise bring separation between God and His people. However, when Jesus' blood was offered on the mercy seat, our sins were sealed up or locked up forever. They would never again cause a separation between our God and us. Sins that were atoned for would once and for all time be put away from God's remembrance as far as the East is from the West. This is liberating news since the result of sin brings death or separation from God.

Make Reconciliation for Iniquity

What did God mean by the phrase, "To make reconciliation for iniquity?" *To make reconciliation* is commonly understood by most as "to make atonement for or to cover over with pitch." This also has the connotation of sealing up something. The real question that affects how we interpret this phrase is, "What is meant by iniquity?" The Hebrew word for iniquity is *"Avon,"* which means perversity, depravity, mischief, or moral evil. Whereas sin is a missing of the mark, which deals with the unlawful act itself, iniquity deals with the morality and character that leads to the wrongful act. These words are found together in the same verse many times throughout the Scriptures, not as a means to bring emphasis through repetition but rather to bring clarity through multiple, varied distinctions.

A sin is an act of missing God's mark; iniquity is evidence of a corrupt nature and morality within the sinner that led to the sin. The word *iniquity* comes from "inequity" and it refers to that which is unequal, unfair, or unjust in our dealings with others, be it with our fellow man or God.

A biblical example which would contrast the difference between sin and iniquity would be the story of David and Bathsheba. David sinned by missing the mark of God's law that explicitly stated that one should not commit adultery with another man's wife, and one should not murder. His iniquity, though, was that of dealing unequally with Uriah, Bathsheba's husband. Uriah demonstrated godly character toward David by serving his king with great loyalty and integrity. David returned Uriah's loyalty with treachery and depravity by having Uriah murdered in battle. However, what more significant example of iniquity (in-equity) has ever been seen than that which is seen in the Righteous One suffering and dying for the unrighteous. Jesus healed the sick, cleansed the lepers, raised the dead, and cast out demons during His earthly ministry, and in return the crowds of people shouted out, "Crucify him, crucify him."

Iniquity can also be resident within God's people. It often happens in a worship service when one is outwardly worshipping God but inwardly his heart is far from God. This inequality between the outward demonstration and the inward intention is iniquity.

> [13]Therefore the Lord said: "Inasmuch as these people draw near with their mouths And honor Me with their lips, But have removed their hearts far from Me, And their fear toward Me is taught by the commandment of men. —Isaiah 29:13

Another good verse that embodies this principle of iniquity was spoken by the prophet, Ezekiel.

> [31]So they come to you as people do, they sit before you as My people, and they hear your words, but they do not do them; for with their mouth they show much love, but their hearts pursue their own gain.
>
> —Ezekiel 33:31

Bring in Everlasting Righteousness

What did God mean by the phrase, "To bring in everlasting righteousness?" The Hebrew word for "to bring in" is *bow*, and some of the meanings of this word are: "to bring in, cause to come in, bring near, and bring to pass." Notice that the essence of this verb is causative or passive in nature. It indicates that the act following the verb is caused to happen for the recipient rather than done by the recipient. The Psalmist often asked God to cause some good thing to occur in his life, rather than depending on his own ability to make it happen. Some examples of this principle would be: "Cause me to hear your loving kindness in the morning for in you I put my trust," or "Open my eyes, that I may behold wonderful things from Your Law," or "Take away reproach and contempt from me," or "Make me understand the way of Your precepts." In Psalm 119, I have counted at least sixty-five times where David asked the Lord to do for him what he was unable to do for himself. My point in all of this is that righteousness is caused by God's actions, not man's.

Notice the keywords in the first three of the six things to be accomplished in the seventy weeks (transgressions, sins, and iniquity) describe man's nature. However, the last three of the six (righteousness, vision/prophecy, and Holy of Holies) have to do with God's nature. The point I want to make is that if man ceased his transgressions, sins, and iniquities, it does change his nature into God's nature. Righteousness is not the cessation of sin, it is the opposite of sin. The same is true of transgressions and iniquities. The only one who can bring in everlasting righteousness is God, Himself, in the person of Jesus Christ.

> [21]For He made Him who knew no sin to be sin for us, that we might become the righteousness of God in Him.
>
> —2 Corinthians 5:21

I want to make it indelibly clear that righteousness cannot be attained by man's determined will or good deed. It is a gift clearly given by God to man.

> [17]For if by the one man's offense death reigned through the one, much more those who receive abundance of grace and of the gift of righteousness will reign in life through the One, Jesus Christ.) [18]Therefore, as through one man's offense judgment came to all men, resulting in condemnation, even so through one Man's righteous act the free gift came to all men, resulting in justification of life. —Romans 5:17-18

Does man have any responsibility concerning righteousness? The answer is, "Yes!" Paul, the apostle, made clear to the saints at Rome that man's responsibility concerning righteousness is to appropriate and receive it as a gift by faith.

> [3]For what does the Scripture say? "ABRAHAM BELIEVED GOD, AND IT WAS ACCOUNTED TO HIM FOR RIGHTEOUSNESS." [4]Now to him who works, the wages are not counted as grace but as debt. [5]But to him who does not work but believes on Him who justifies the ungodly, his faith is accounted for righteousness, [6]just as David also describes the blessedness of the man to whom God imputes righteousness apart from works: [7]"BLESSED ARE THOSE WHOSE LAWLESS DEEDS ARE FORGIVEN, AND WHOSE SINS ARE COVERED; [8]BLESSED IS THE MAN TO WHOM THE LORD SHALL NOT IMPUTE SIN." —Romans 4:3-8

Let's not make the same mistake that much of Israel did by trying to go about establishing our own righteousness. It is indeed a very fatal error with fatal consequences.

> [3]For they being ignorant of God's righteousness, and seeking to establish their own righteousness, have not submitted to the righteousness of God. [4]For Christ is the end of the law for righteousness to everyone who believes. —Romans 10:3-4

Only Jesus can bring in everlasting righteousness. As the everlasting God, He came, took on flesh, and became the eternal sacrifice for our unrighteousness, that we who receive this gift of righteousness might have eternal life with Him.

> [12]But this Man, after He had offered one sacrifice for sins forever, sat down at the right hand of God, [13]from that time waiting till His enemies are made His footstool. [14]For by one offering He has perfected forever those who are being sanctified. —Hebrews 10:12-14

Seal Up Vision and Prophecy

What did God mean by the phrase, "To seal up vision and prophecy?" The same Hebrew word, *Chatham*, that was used in sealing or locking up sin earlier in this verse is used here in this phrase. It indicates sealing something so it can be opened only by the one who has the key that will open the seal, as seen in Isaiah 29:11.

> [11]The whole vision has become to you like the words of a book that is sealed, which men deliver to one who is literate, saying, "Read this, please." And he says, "I cannot, for it is sealed." —Isaiah 29:11

What was to be sealed up? Most translations say to seal up vision and prophecy, but let's take a look at the Hebrew word for *prophecy*. The word is *nabiy*, which means "prophet," not "prophecy." So this phrase now reads, "To seal up the vision and the prophet." To understand what Gabriel was saying to Daniel, we need to identify the vision and the prophet. To do this, it is imperative that we look at the context leading up to Gabriel's statement.

Concerning the vision that is being spoken of, it is relatively simple to identify when you recognize that Daniel had received one dream in chapter seven and one vision in chapter eight leading up to this encounter with Gabriel. Daniel did not understand the vision of chapter eight, and neither did anyone else to whom he told it. The vision was a basic timeline of prophetic events that extended from Daniel's day to the end of the age. Daniel was troubled by the vision and was surely inquiring of the Lord as to its meaning.

> [26]"And the vision of the evenings and mornings Which was told is true; Therefore seal up the vision, For it refers to many days in the future. [27]And I, Daniel, fainted and was sick for days; afterward, I arose and went about the king's business. I was astonished by the vision, but no one understood it. —Daniel 8:26-27

Daniel saw this vision shortly before Babylon fell to the Medes and Persians, after which he was relocated to the palace of Shushan in Persia. In chapter nine, which was the first year of King Darius' reign, Daniel was studying the books and, in particular, the prophecy of Jeremiah. He understood from the prophecy that the time of Israel's captivity and the desolations of Jerusalem were coming to an end. Daniel began to cry out to God concerning this matter while confessing that God's judgments were just and justified. While he was praying, Gabriel appeared to him about the time of the evening oblation. He told Daniel that God had sent him to give him an understanding of the matter he was considering (Jeremiah's prophecy) and about the troublesome vision he had received in Daniel, chapter 9.

> 21yes, while I was speaking in prayer, the man Gabriel, whom I had seen in the vision at the beginning, being caused to fly swiftly, reached me about the time of the evening offering. 22And he informed me, and talked with me, and said, "O Daniel, I have now come forth to give you skill to understand. 23At the beginning of your supplications the command went out, and I have come to tell you, for you are greatly beloved; therefore consider the matter, and understand the vision:
>
> —Daniel 9:21-23

Notice that Daniel was given understanding concerning the question he had been considering (Jeremiah's prophecy) and concerning the vision he had previously seen.

Now let's focus our attention again on the phrase, "Seal up vision and the prophet." The purpose of a seal was not only to lock up or hide the contents of a scroll from those to whom it was not intended but also to authenticate the messenger and the message as being sent from the one whose seal was on the manuscript. God's seal was a validation of the prophet and a confirmation of the vision. Once a letter is sealed, its contents are irreversible – Daniel 6:8. It locks up both until the time appointed and is only to be opened by those who are selected.

This sealing or spiritual blindness was to be especially relevant to the nation of Israel who would reject their Messiah's coming and miss the day of their visitation. Look at the following Scriptures:

> [25]For I do not desire, brethren, that you should be ignorant of this mystery, lest you should be wise in your own opinion, that blindness in part has happened to Israel until the fullness of the Gentiles has come in.
>
> —Romans 11:25

> [18]having their understanding darkened, being alienated from the life of God, because of the ignorance that is in them, because of the blindness of their heart.
>
> —Ephesians 4:18

Israel's blindness was a part of God's judgment for failing the second 490-year test when they rejected their Messiah, even though God told them the very year He would come to them. They were also blinded to the seventy-week prophecy that was about them alone. This prophecy was not concerning the Gentiles. This blindness concerning their Messiah will remain in place for the nation for the rest of this age. It will be removed at Christ's second coming to usher in the millennial kingdom (read Zechariah, chapters 12-14).

> [13]unlike Moses, who put a veil over his face so that the
> children of Israel could not look steadily at the end of
> what was passing away. [14]But their minds were blinded.
> For until this day, the same veil remains unlifted in the
> reading of the Old Testament because the veil is taken
> away in Christ. [15]But even to this day, when Moses is
> read, a veil lies on their heart. [16]Nevertheless, when one
> turns to the Lord, the veil is taken away.
>
> —2 Corinthians 3:13-16

God has sovereignly chosen to hide some of His end-time prophetic intentions in the cloak of mystery for all nations. God intends to reveal what has been a hidden mystery for many years at an appointed time near the end of the age. I believe God will put it on the hearts of some to whom it is appointed to diligently search for an understanding of these mysteries.

> [2]It is the glory of God to conceal a matter, But the glory of kings is to search out a matter. —Proverbs 25:2

I believe it will be the destiny of some in the last days to have their eyes divinely opened to understand the mysteries which have been hidden and sealed for centuries. These people will be able to unlock the mysteries because they will be appointed by God, not because they will be wiser or more spiritual than scholars of previous generations. It is merely a matter of God's timing and purpose. Could we be part of the terminal generation at the end of the age that will be given the keys to unlock these mysteries? Considering the many prophetic end-time signs unfolding, it is not only possible but probable.

Anoint the Most Holy

What did God mean by the phrase, "To anoint the Most Holy?" *To anoint* means "to consecrate after its pollution." It is interesting that in the Hebrew the same word, "Qodesh," is used twice consecutively and means holy, holiness, set-apartness. When a word is used twice back to back, it is for emphasis, such as, "Truly, truly, I say unto you." The emphasis is placed on the first word. This phrase would then read, "to anoint the holiest of holies."

There are several schools of thought as to what is being referred to as the holiest of the holies. One view is that the phrase speaks of a place such as the Holy of Holies in the temple. Those who hold this view believe this passage of Scripture is referring to anointing the Holy of Holies of a rebuilt temple in Jerusalem. I personally don't think there will be a rebuilt temple in this age, although I believe there will be in the millennial kingdom. Another less popular view is that this phrase speaks of a person. I am persuaded that the less popular opinion is what is being referred to in this passage. When the Holy Spirit comes to anoint the holiest of holies, I believe He will choose a person over a place. Though the Holy of Holies is the most sacred place in the temple, I believe Jesus, the Messiah, is the eternal holiest of all the holies. He professed that He was a temple.

> 19Jesus answered and said to them, "Destroy this temple,
> and in three days, I will raise it up." 20Then the Jews said,
> "It has taken forty-six years to build this temple, and will
> You raise it up in three days?" 21But He was speaking of

> the temple of His body. [22]Therefore, when He had risen from the dead, His disciples remembered that He had said this to them; and they believed the Scripture and the word which Jesus had said. —John 2:19-22

As a matter of fact, any rebuilt temple in Jerusalem will only be temporal. Revelation chapter twenty-one states that there will be no temple in the New Jerusalem of the eternal state.

> [22]But I saw no temple in it, for the Lord God Almighty and the Lamb are its temple. [23]The city had no need of the sun or of the moon to shine in it, for the glory of God illuminated it. The Lamb is its light.
>
> —Revelation 21:22-23

Another reason I am convinced that this anointing refers to Jesus is that the period in which this anointing occurs happens within the seventy weeks prophesied over Israel. Any rebuilt temple will not exist until after the seventy weeks have concluded. Daniel was told these six things would be accomplished in the seventy weeks. The question then is, "Who will accomplish these?"

CHAPTER 8

A MEASURING STICK FOR ISRAEL

The Misappropriation of the Daniel 9:24-27 Prophecy

Many Bible teachers have used this seventy-week prophecy to establish and give basis for a considerable amount of their eschatological doctrine. I am entirely convinced that in its purest intent, this prophecy has everything to do with the course of Israel for the half-century following Daniel's receiving of it. It takes us through the coming of the Messiah, to His death, burial, and resurrection, and to the destruction of Jerusalem and scattering of Israel in 70 AD. Though the effects of this prophecy were intact long after its fulfillment, there is no mention of Israel's future in this prophecy after its dispersion. Indeed other prophecies clearly speak of Israel's prophetic future, such as her being regathered as a nation to Israel and the return of the holy city, Jerusalem, into her possession. This prophecy is not at all eschatological. I know this is somewhat of a shocking statement, especially since many of the teachings on eschatology have cited this prophecy as a significant proof text.

Having said this, I do believe that this prophecy has typological relevance to how the end of this age will unfold. Before I explain what I mean by this in the next section, let me first make clear that I do not believe in replacement theology like some. Some embrace the replacement theology concept, believing that the prophecies of the Old Testament which were intended for the Jews are now destined for the Church because of Israel's unbelief. Many Christians posture themselves as though all the judgments of the Old Testament are relative to the Jews but are quick to claim all the blessed promises for themselves, the Church. I do not believe that Israel's failures changed the benefactor-ship of the promises of God. One day God will graft the natural branches that were cut off back into the tree into which the believing Gentiles were grafted (read Romans 11:7-32). However, the rebellion of Israel has cost and will continue to cost her dearly. The prophecy we are studying declares this to be true. I believe that her disobedience has resulted in being cut off from God the rest of this age as the tool of choice to forward the kingdom of God on this earth. By the tool of God's choice, I mean the calling as a royal priesthood to take the kingdom of God to the whole world. In that sense, the Church has replaced her in this age, as in 1 Peter 2:5-10.

> [5]...you also, as living stones, are being built up a spiritual house, a holy priesthood, to offer up spiritual sacrifices

> acceptable to God through Jesus Christ. [6]Therefore it is also contained in the Scripture, "BEHOLD, I LAY IN ZION A CHIEF CORNERSTONE, ELECT, PRECIOUS, AND HE WHO BELIEVES ON HIM WILL BY NO MEANS BE PUT TO SHAME." [7]Therefore, to you who believe, He is precious; but to those who are disobedient, "THE STONE WHICH THE BUILDERS REJECTED HAS BECOME THE CHIEF CORNERSTONE," [8]and "A STONE OF STUMBLING AND A ROCK OF OFFENSE." They stumble, being disobedient to the word, to which they also were appointed. [9]But you are a chosen generation, a royal priesthood, a holy nation, His own special people, that you may proclaim the praises of Him who called you out of darkness into His marvelous light; [10]who once were not a people but are now the people of God, who had not obtained mercy but now have obtained mercy.
>
> —1 Peter 2:5-10

However, in the millennial kingdom, Israel will once again be offered the priesthood and once again become the tool of God's choice to cause the kingdom of God to fill the earth. As a punishment for failing their second 490-year test in a little over a thousand years, God inflicted spiritual blindness upon them that exists to this very day.

> [7]What then? Israel has not obtained what it seeks, but the elect have obtained it, and the rest were blinded. [8]Just as it is written: "GOD HAS GIVEN THEM A SPIRIT OF STUPOR, EYES THAT THEY SHOULD NOT SEE AND EARS THAT THEY SHOULD NOT HEAR, TO THIS VERY DAY." [9]And

> David says: "LET THEIR TABLE BECOME A SNARE AND A TRAP, A STUMBLING BLOCK AND A RECOMPENSE TO THEM. 10LET THEIR EYES BE DARKENED, SO THAT THEY DO NOT SEE, AND BOW DOWN THEIR BACK ALWAYS."
>
> —Romans 11:7-10

This blindness is not lifted until they see Him whom they have pierced at His second coming with His saints at the end of this age (read the prophecy of Zechariah chapters 12-14).

The Spiritual Relevance and Benefit of this Prophecy

Now let's pick up again the idea of this prophecy serving as a typological hint as to what is to come for the Church in this age. Often prophecy has a dual interpretation as to its fulfillment. I explained this in great detail in Section 1 of my previous book, *The Terminal Generation.* There I elaborate that a prophecy can have one or more typological fulfillments but only one ultimate fulfillment. An example of this would be prophecies concerning God's house or dwelling place. In the wilderness, the tabernacle served only as a typological prophetic fulfillment of God's ultimate intention of the house in which He would one day dwell. Likewise, the same is true of the tabernacle of David, the temple of Solomon, the rebuilt temple of Nehemiah, and Herod's temple in the days of Jesus. All of these were types and shadows of the true temple or house that God had in mind from the very beginning. He said the house to which He was prophetically referring was not one that man would build Him but one that He, Himself, would build out of living stones. It is interesting to note that the ultimate prophetic fulfillment of a prophecy for Israel can many times serve as a typological fulfillment for the Church. An example of this principle can be seen in Exodus 19 where God offers a prophetic promise to Israel of being priests of the Most High God, that the earth might be filled with the glory of God's kingdom. This offer was not to just to the Levites but instead was an offer of priesthood for the entire, holy (separated) nation.

> [4]'You have seen what I did to the Egyptians, and how I bore you on eagles' wings and brought you to Myself. [5]Now, therefore, if you will indeed obey My voice and keep My covenant, then you shall be a special treasure to Me above all people; for all the earth is Mine. [6]And you shall be to Me a kingdom of priests and a holy nation.' These are the words which you shall speak to the children of Israel." —Exodus 19:4-6

When Moses presented God's prophetic promise to Israel, they said they were agreeable with the terms and would come into prophetic alignment with God. Moses then relayed their answer to God who, upon hearing, sent back the following communique to His people through Moses.

> [9]And the LORD said to Moses, "Behold, I come to you in the thick cloud, that the people may hear when I speak with you and believe you forever." So Moses told the words of the people to the LORD. [10]Then the LORD said to Moses, "Go to the people and consecrate them today and tomorrow, and let them wash their clothes. [11]And let

> them be ready for the third day. For on the third day the LORD will come down upon Mount Sinai in the sight of all the people. —Exodus 19:9-11

The rest is history. When Israel met with God on the third day, they were so terrified of His presence that they told Moses that they did not want the privilege of standing in His presence and hearing His voice directly. They wanted someone to mediate His direct presence and voice. In essence, they rejected the priesthood that God had prophetically promised them. Hebrews chapter twelve records God's angry response to them while warning the Church not to make the same mistake of rejecting God's ultimate prophetic promise. Because of their rejection, God established an inferior priesthood within the nation that reflected their desires. It is referred to as the Levitical priesthood in which only one of the twelve tribes would be allowed to participate. In this priesthood, only the high priest was granted the privilege of standing in the presence of God and hearing His voice directly, and this was limited to one time per year. This priesthood was a mere typological fulfillment of the initial offer which one day Israel will ultimately see fulfilled during the millennial kingdom. Israel's initial prophetic promise is a type and shadow of the priesthood that has since been promised to the Church.

With these principles in mind, let's revisit the statement I made earlier, "I believe that this prophecy has typological relevance to how the end of this age will unfold." Though I am not a proponent of replacement theology, I do believe

Israel's history is a divine pattern of what will become the history of the Church. If we know how God worked with and related to those He called to be His children in the past, we know what we can expect from God as He works with and relates to us, His children, today. Not only are the destinies and means to attain them the same, so also will God's ultimate plan of spending eternity in the presence of the Lord be the same for all. Hebrews 13:8 says that Jesus is the same yesterday, today, and forever. He is not a respecter of children, and He is the Lord God who changes not. The same destiny and testing process to inherit it that the first Adam was subjected to is also the same to which the Second Adam (Jesus) was subjected. Paul, the apostle, made it very clear to the Church that she should learn from Israel's history so as not to repeat it. Her history also served as an example of what to expect for their own future. The following Scriptures should soundly convince the reader of this.

> [4]For whatever things were written before were written for our learning, that we through the patience and comfort of the Scriptures might have hope.
>
> —Romans 15:4

> [11]Now all these things happened to them as examples, and they were written for our admonition, upon whom the ends of the ages have come. —1 Corinthians 10:11

In this last verse, it should read, "Upon whom the end of the age has come." The Greek word for ages in the NKJV refers to an age or space of time. Paul is saying that the history of Israel and how God worked with His people in the past serves as a schematic of how the end of the church age will unfold.

The Primary Purpose of This Prophecy

What was God's purpose for this seventy-week prophecy? Though He was prophesying about many things that would happen in Israel's future, the primary intended objective was to give Israel a precise measuring instrument to one of the most important events of her prophetic destiny. I am referring specifically to the time of the coming of her Messiah to bring salvation to Israel and even to the Gentiles. The proof that the Jews and her leaders were using this as a prophetic measuring stick is evidenced by the following Scripture.

> [15]Now as the people were in expectation, and all reasoned in their hearts about John, whether he was the Christ or not, [16]John answered, saying to all, "I indeed baptize you with water; but One mightier than I is coming, whose sandal strap I am not worthy to loose. He will baptize you with the Holy Spirit and fire.
>
> —Luke 3:15-16

Notice that the people of Israel were in expectation to the point that they were wondering if John was the Christ for whom they were looking. Though John made it clear he was not, he also made it clear that the one coming after him was. When John was further quizzed as to who he was, he spoke clearly as to who he was and what his mission was.

> [19]Now, this is the testimony of John, when the Jews sent priests and Levites from Jerusalem to ask him, "Who are you?" [20]He confessed, and did not deny, but confessed, "I am not the Christ." [21]And they asked him, "What then? Are you Elijah?" He said, "I am not." "Are you the Prophet?" And he answered, "No." [22]Then they said to him, "Who are you, that we may give an answer to those who sent us? What do you say about yourself?" [23]He said: "I am 'THE VOICE OF ONE CRYING IN THE WILDERNESS: "MAKE STRAIGHT THE WAY OF THE LORD,"' as the prophet Isaiah said."
>
> —John 1:19-23

The above quote is from Isaiah 40:3-5. The final verse of this passage was that he would cause the glory of the Lord to be revealed and that all flesh would see it together. It is interesting to note that on more than one occasion the Jews, Pharisees, Sadducees, priests, and scribes must have suspected John might be the Messiah as they indeed were not bashful about asking him directly. This is another proof that many in Israel knew it was the right season for the Messiah's arrival and that they were looking to see who it might be. After John met Jesus, the One who was to come after him, he unapologetically declared that Jesus was the Son of God.

> [29]The next day John saw Jesus coming toward him, and said, "Behold! The Lamb of God who takes away the sin of the world [30]This is He of whom I said, 'After me comes a Man who is preferred before me, for He was before me.' [31]I did not know Him; but that He should be revealed to Israel, therefore I came baptizing with water." [32]And John bore witness, saying, "I saw the Spirit descending

> from heaven like a dove, and He remained upon Him.
> 33I did not know Him, but He who sent me to baptize with water said to me, 'Upon whom you see the Spirit descending, and remaining on Him, this is He who baptizes with the Holy Spirit.' 34And I have seen and testified that this is the Son of God." —John 1:29-34

Even thirty years before John's ministry, God prophetically declared that Jesus was the Messiah, who was to come. He did this shortly after His birth. At His birth, the angels announced to the shepherds: today, there was born a Savior, who is Christ the Lord. And then shortly after His birth, we see two individuals publicly testifying in the temple that Jesus was the Christ for whom they were looking (see Luke chapter two). The first was Simeon, who was promised by God that he would not die until he saw the Lord's Christ. When he saw Jesus' parents bring Him into the temple, he blessed the Child and then asked the Lord to let him die for his eyes had seen God's salvation. At the same time, the second witness, Anna, came forth to confirm that Jesus was the Redeemer.

I am belaboring this point because I want you to see that many in Israel were expecting their Messiah because they understood how to use the precise measuring stick of the seventy-week prophecy of Daniel. This prophecy declared that it would be precisely 483 years from the decree to rebuild Jerusalem to the coming of the Messiah. It was on the minds of many in Israel because they knew how to count and, therefore, were totally yearning for and expecting their Messiah to come and deliver them.

In addition to these I have discussed, some others confessed He was the Christ, the Messiah, throughout His ministry. Let's take a look at some other examples that also leave Israel without excuse for missing the day of their visitation.

In John 1, we see that Andrew and Simon Peter confessed Jesus as the Messiah, which is translated "the Christ."

> [40]One of the two who heard John speak, and followed Him, was Andrew, Simon Peter's brother. [41]He first found his own brother Simon, and said to him, "We have found the Messiah" (which is translated, the Christ).
>
> —John 1:40-41

Also, in John 1, we see Philip and Nathaniel receiving this same revelation.

> [45]Philip found Nathanael and said to him, "We have found Him of whom Moses in the law, and also the prophets, wrote—Jesus of Nazareth, the son of Joseph."
> [46]And Nathanael said to him, "Can anything good come out of Nazareth?" Philip said to him, "Come and see."
> [47]Jesus saw Nathanael coming toward Him, and said of him, "Behold, an Israelite indeed, in whom is no deceit!"
> [48]Nathanael said to Him, "How do You know me?" Jesus answered and said to him, "Before Philip called you when you were under the fig tree, I saw you." [49]Nathanael answered and said to Him, "Rabbi, You are the Son of God! You are the King of Israel!"
>
> —John 1:45-49

In Matthew 16, Jesus asked His disciples who they thought He was, and Peter answered correctly.

> 15He said to them, "But who do you say that I am?"
> 16Simon Peter answered and said, "You are the Christ,
> the Son of the living God." 17Jesus answered and said
> to him, "Blessed are you, Simon Bar-Jonah, for flesh and
> blood has not revealed this to you, but My Father who
> is in heaven. —Matthew 16:15-17

Many of the common-folk Jews who witnessed His teachings and the miraculous ministry believed He was the Messiah in spite of their spiritual leaders confessing the contrary.

> 26But look! He speaks boldly, and they say nothing to
> Him. Do the rulers know indeed that this is truly the
> Christ? 27However, we know where this Man is from;
> but when the Christ comes, no one knows where He
> is from." 31And many of the people believed in Him, and
> said, "When the Christ comes, will He do more signs
> than these which this Man has done?"
> —John 7:26-27, 31

And now follows some very damning evidence against the religious elite of Israel.

Very early in the ministry of Christ, even a Samaritan woman and other Samaritans that she witnessed to believed that Jesus was the Messiah. Let us not forget that Samaritans were considered by the Jews to be half-breeds and spiritually inferior.

> 29"Come, see a Man who told me all things that I ever
> did. Could this be the Christ?" 42Then they said to the

> woman, "Now we believe, not because of what you said, for we ourselves have heard Him and we know that this is indeed the Christ, the Savior of the world."
>
> —John 4:29, 42

And not only that, but even the demons on more than one occasion knew who Jesus was and confessed Him as the Christ, the Son of God. Here is one of those examples.

> 28When he saw Jesus, he cried out, fell down before Him, and with a loud voice said, "What have I to do with You, Jesus, Son of the Highest God? I beg You, do not torment me!"
>
> —Luke 8:28

Finally, last but certainly not least, is Jesus' own testimony and confession of who He was, before His people who should have known.

> 24Then the Jews surrounded Him and said to Him, "How long do You keep us in doubt? If You are the Christ, tell us plainly." 25Jesus answered them, "I told you, and you do not believe. The works that I do in My Father's name, they bear witness of Me. 26But you do not believe, because you are not of My sheep, as I said to you. 27My sheep hear My voice, and I know them, and they follow Me. 28And I give them eternal life, and they shall never perish; neither shall anyone snatch them out of My hand. 29My Father, who has given them to Me, is greater than all; and no one is able to snatch them out of My Father's hand. 30I and My Father are one."
>
> —John 10:24-30

Jesus even made His confession before the High Priest of Israel when he put Jesus under oath by the living God as to whether He was the Christ.

> [63]But Jesus kept silent. And the high priest answered and said to Him, "I put You under oath by the living God: Tell us if You are the Christ, the Son of God!" [64]Jesus said to him, "It is as you said. Nevertheless, I say to you, hereafter you will see the Son of Man sitting at the right hand of the Power, and coming on the clouds of heaven."
>
> —Matthew 26:63-64

I trust that the above examples offer you, the reader, sufficient proof that the people of Israel were in fact in a state of expectancy and hope for the coming of their Messiah. The prophetic measuring stick that Daniel gave the nation was the very reason for their expectation. If they knew the year and season of their Messiah's coming, the question that should have arisen was, "If Jesus isn't the one, then who is?" Even to this day, long past the 483 years, the Jews are still looking for their Messiah to come. The fact is that He has come and they missed it. The good news is that He will come again, and they will see and recognize Him whom they have pierced.

CHAPTER 9

THE PROPHECY'S UNFOLDING

The Unfolding of this Prophecy

Now I would like to focus on the unfolding of the six things that Daniel said would be accomplished within the seventy weeks. Verse 24 of Daniel nine lists them, but verses 25-27 expound on their fulfillment. Let us now look at a verse by verse expository rendering of their fulfillment.

Daniel 9:25

In verses 25-27, Daniel basically divides the seventy-week prophecy into three partitions based on when these various end-time events would happen. In verse 25, we see the first two partitions.

> 25"Know therefore and understand, That from the going forth of the command To restore and build Jerusalem

> Until Messiah the Prince, There shall be seven weeks and sixty-two weeks; The street shall be built again, and the wall, Even in troublesome times. —Daniel 9:25

Notice the two partitions identified in this verse are seven weeks, followed by sixty-two weeks. These cover sixty-nine of the seventy weeks that Daniel prophesied. The first partition spans 49 years and the second spans 434 years. The two total 483 years of the 490-year prophecy. The 49-year segment has to do with the length of time it would take for the rebuilding project and the establishment of an orderly way of life that had ceased some seventy years prior. It also served notice that they would experience resistance from those residing in their homeland and that the rebuilding process would take place in troublesome times. There is nothing said about the next sixty-two weeks as concerning what significant events would take place. I personally believe that the 434-year period after the rebuilding was finished signifies a period in which Israel was to patiently wait for the seventieth and final week to begin during which most of what was prophesied would take place. The most significant piece of information to glean from this verse is that from the going forth of the command to restore and build Jerusalem until Messiah, the Prince, there shall be seven weeks and sixty-two weeks (69 weeks or 483 years).

As I shared in the previous chapter, this prophecy was to provide Israel the ability to understand an ordained precise measurement of time so that they might know the exact year that their Messiah, the Prince, would come to them. Again,

I believe this supports the notion that Israel was fully anticipating the arrival of their Messiah at the time of Jesus' actual coming. I feel they missed their day of visitation because they were expecting Him to come as a conquering King and not a lowly servant. John chapter one says that Jesus came to His own, but His own received Him not. Why? Because Jesus did not fit the narrative they had embraced. They had a stereotyped concept of what the fulfillment of this prophecy would look like when it occurred, and apparently, Jesus did not feel at all obligated to accommodate their preconceived expectations or teachings.

Concerning the decree spoken of in this verse, there is much dispute. The argument centers on whether the decree had to do with the rebuilding of the city, the walls, the temple or a combination of building one while finishing the other. There are four decrees listed in the Scriptures with scholars favoring one or the other for various reasons. Below are the four decrees with their Scriptural references:

Four possible decrees:

1. 537 BC — Ezra 1
2. 520 BC — Ezra 6
3. 457 BC — Ezra 7
4. 444 BC — Nehemiah 2

As to which one to embrace as the fulfillment of verse 25, I would choose the third (457 BC). This choice is not based on what is being rebuilt but rather is based on timing.

Historically speaking, we know the timing of John the Baptist's baptizing of the Messiah as well as the approximate time of Jesus' birth. Most place the birth of Christ at or near 4 BC. Given the generally accepted age of 30 for Jesus at His baptism (Luke 3:23) and that this baptism occurred in the 15th year of Tiberius (Luke 3:1), this date would seem to be reasonably accurate. On this basis, the Fall season of 27 AD would be the time of His baptism. Considering this, only one of the decrees even remotely fits the timing of Daniel's prophecy. The decree to which I am speaking is the 3rd decree given in Ezra 7, which took place in the Fall of 457 BC. The others are either too early or too late to be in sync with that which Daniel was referencing. The Ezra 7:23-26 decree was about permitting civil and religious autonomy to be restored in Jerusalem in compliance with God's law. This would satisfy the letter of Daniel's prophecy. If, indeed, the Fall of 457 BC is the date that Daniel was referring to in the seventy-week prophecy, this would place the coming of the Messiah in the Fall of 27 AD. Some scholars place His coming as the day of His baptism when John confessed that He was the Messiah. Others hold to a time shortly after that when Jesus acknowledges Himself to be the Anointed One. My personal belief would be the sure confession by Jesus after having returned from the wilderness testing. Upon His return, Jesus went into the synagogue on the Sabbath day to read. He was given the book of Isaiah to read. He opened to Luke 4:16-21.

> 16So He came to Nazareth, where He had been brought up. And as His custom was, He went into the synagogue

> on the Sabbath day and stood up to read. [17]And He was handed the book of the prophet Isaiah. And when He had opened the book, He found the place where it was written: [18]"THE SPIRIT OF THE LORD IS UPON ME BECAUSE HE HAS ANOINTED ME TO PREACH THE GOSPEL TO THE POOR; HE HAS SENT ME TO HEAL THE BROKENHEARTED, TO PROCLAIM LIBERTY TO THE CAPTIVES AND RECOVERY OF SIGHT TO THE BLIND, TO SET AT LIBERTY THOSE WHO ARE OPPRESSED; [19]TO PROCLAIM THE ACCEPTABLE YEAR OF THE LORD." [20]Then He closed the book, and gave it back to the attendant and sat down. And the eyes of all who were in the synagogue were fixed on Him. [21]And He began to say to them, "Today this Scripture is fulfilled in your hearing." —Luke 4:16-21

This Scripture speaks to His being anointed by God. Upon finishing His reading, He declared, "This Day, This Scripture" is fulfilled in the hearing of God's people. It is important to note that Jesus' coming as Israel's Messiah did not happen until sixty-nine of the seventy weeks were completed. As we continue our study of this prophecy, this fact becomes paramount in establishing our doctrine as to what happens during the seventieth week and when it happens.

In Daniel 9:26, three main points are highlighted.

> [26]"And after the sixty-two weeks Messiah shall be cut off, but not for Himself; And the people of the prince who is to come Shall destroy the city and the sanctuary. The end of it shall be with a flood, And till the end of the war, desolations are determined. —Daniel 9:26

The three points are as follows:

1. After the sixty-two weeks, the Messiah shall be cut off, but not for Himself.
2. The people of the prince who is to come shall destroy the city and the sanctuary.
3. The end of it shall be with a flood, and till the end of the war, desolations are determined.

Now let us cover each point in more detail.

Point One:

Daniel says that the Messiah (Jesus) would be cut off after the sixty-two weeks which follows the first 7 weeks to rebuild the temple. Therefore, the timing of this event is after the sixty-ninth week has concluded. This fact leaves us with one of only two options. Option one would be that this event took place between the sixty-ninth and seventieth week. Option two would be that this event took place during the seventieth week. I will cover these options in more detail later in this chapter. Now let's look at the event that took place. Daniel said that the Messiah would be cut off, but not for Himself. I am fully persuaded this is clearly speaking of the crucifixion of Jesus, at which time His earthly ministry was cut off. This fact brought an end for the need for animal sacrifices for atonement. He goes on to say that it was not for His benefit. I believe the benefactors are all those who through faith would believe in Him and what He accomplished through His sacrificial death, burial, and resurrection. These would include saints who through faith looked ahead to the prophetic fulfillment of the atonement as well as those who through faith look back on the historical fulfillment of Christ's atonement.

Point Two:

In this point, Daniel says that the people of the prince who is to come shall destroy the city and the sanctuary. Some scholars think the prince being referred to is the Antichrist. I am not of that persuasion at all. I believe it is referring to the Romans serving under the Roman general, Titus, who in 70 AD utterly destroyed Jerusalem and the temple. This was the fulfillment of the prophecy Jesus spoke of to His disciples about a day that was coming when not one stone would be left on top of another in the temple. He also prophesied of this time of destruction as He wept over Jerusalem and the people for their spiritual blindness. This blindness would result in Israel missing the day of her visitation and peace.

Point Three:

The third point Daniel made in this verse is that the end of this siege, spoken of in verse 26, would come like a flood, and that every desolation God prophetically determined would be accomplished before this war ended. Again, I do not think this is about an end-time prophetic event at the end of the age. I believe it was merely giving more detail to the destruction of Jerusalem and the temple in 70 AD. Let's read what was determined when Jesus prophesied of that day in Luke.

> [41]Now as He drew near, He saw the city and wept over it, [42]saying, "If you had known, even you, especially in this your day, the things that make for your peace! But now they are hidden from your eyes. [43]For days will come upon you when your enemies will build an embankment around you, surround you and close you in on every side, [44]and level you, and your children within you, to the ground; and they will not leave in you one stone upon another, because you did not know the time of your visitation."
>
> —Luke 19:41-44

In the final verse of the seventy-week prophecy, Daniel speaks of a covenant being confirmed for one week, the end of the sacrifice in the middle of that week, one would arise that makes desolate, and the duration of this desolation would be until the consummation of what God had determined would be accomplished.

> [27]Then he shall confirm a covenant with many for one week, But in the middle of the week, He shall bring an end to sacrifice and offering. And on the wing of abominations shall be one who makes desolate, Even until the consummation, which is determined, Is poured out on the desolate."
>
> —Daniel 9:27

What was Daniel saying here? Was he speaking prophetically about the destruction at the end of the age when the empire of the Beast under the leadership of the Antichrist and the False Prophet brings devastation to God's people? Or was he giving even more detail about the same event concerning 70 AD? Again, it is my position that none of what

Daniel is prophesying in these verses has to do with the last days of this age in which we are living. Instead, I believe he is speaking about Jesus covenanting Himself to the fulfillment of the seventieth week during which He comes and declares Himself to be their Messiah. We know that His ministry lasted approximately three and one-half years before becoming the eternal sacrifice on Golgotha's hill. When He died, the veil in the temple was ripped asunder from top to bottom, indicating there would be no more blood sacrifices offered in the holy of holies of the physical temple in Jerusalem. Concerning the seventieth week of Daniel, the Savior's earthly ministry spanned half of that time or 3½ years. The apostles continued the work of His ministry for the next 3½ years to the people of Israel, teaching with signs and wonders following that Jesus was indeed the Messiah they had been looking for. At the end of the week, when it was evident that Israel, as a nation, rejected her Messiah and that the window of opportunity (70 weeks) had concluded, Jesus sealed Israel's fate by calling Saul of Tarsus and setting him apart to take the gospel of the kingdom to the Gentiles. The apostles declared the Jews unworthy of the gospel because of their unbelief and subsequently turned their attention to preaching the gospel to the Gentiles. This places the end of the 70 weeks, (490 years) in the fall of 34 AD. This would put the year of the crucifixion, (which happened in the middle of the 70th week of Daniel), in the Spring of 31 AD.

> 45But when the Jews saw the multitudes, they were filled with envy; and contradicting and blaspheming, they opposed the things spoken by Paul. 46Then Paul

> and Barnabas grew bold and said, "It was necessary that the word of God should be spoken to you first; but since you reject it, and judge yourselves unworthy of everlasting life, behold, we turn to the Gentiles. [47]For so the Lord has commanded us: 'I HAVE SET YOU AS A LIGHT TO THE GENTILES, THAT YOU SHOULD BE FOR SALVATION TO THE ENDS OF THE EARTH.' —Acts 13:45-47

If Israel's judgment seems rather severe to you, let me remind you of the reason for God's severity as articulated by Jesus, Himself in Luke 11.

> [47]Woe to you! For you build the tombs of the prophets, and your fathers killed them. [48]In fact, you bear witness that you approve the deeds of your fathers; for they indeed killed them, and you build their tombs. [49]Therefore the wisdom of God also said, 'I will send them prophets and apostles, and some of them they will kill and persecute,' [50]that the blood of all the prophets which was shed from the foundation of the world may be required of this generation, [51]from the blood of Abel to the blood of Zechariah who perished between the altar and the temple. Yes, I say to you, it shall be required of this generation. —Luke11:47-51

Before we conclude this chapter, I would like to address another crucial doctrinal issue concerning Daniel's seventy-week prophecy. I am referring to the teaching by many today that there is a two-thousand-year gap or interval between the 69th and 70th week of Daniel's prophecy.

Church Age Interval Theory

First of all, I want to confess that I both embraced and taught this as a part of my eschatological doctrine for years, until the Lord challenged me several years ago. I had even included this theory as a fact in some of the discipleship curriculum I had written previously.

While preparing to teach on this subject several years ago, I heard the Lord say to me, "On what scriptural basis and by what spiritual authority do you teach that there are two-thousand years between the 69th and 70th week of Daniel's prophecy?" The voice seemed so clear and challenging. At first, I was dumbfounded. I reasoned within myself as to whether or not this was actually God or an attempt by the enemy to question sound doctrine. In the days and weeks ahead, I scoured the Scriptures like a Berean to see if what I had been taught and had been teaching myself was of God. I felt like a man on a mission to prove once and for all if it was true or not. I told the Lord that I was open to either result.

It was at this point that I began to consider the basis of why I taught this concept the way I had. I couldn't remember a time that I had seriously studied and received spiritual insights from the Scriptures or from my inquiring of the Lord on this matter. I realized I taught it because it was what I was taught and consequently assumed to be true. This should not be the basis on which a Bible teacher instructs the Word of God.

As I continued to search for proof texts, I came up empty-handed. I began to realize that I had no basis for teaching such a doctrine. As a matter of fact, I started to see that this doctrine created some problematic theological questions that I could not answer. In the following paragraphs, I would like to enumerate and discuss some of these.

The first question I could not answer was, "What Scriptures declare there would be a two-thousand-year gap between week 69 and week 70?" I couldn't find one. God impressed on me that the prophecy was to provide Israel with a precise measuring stick to know the exact year of their Messiah's coming so they would not miss the day of their visitation. I began to reason that between week-one and week-two, there were precisely seven years. Between week-two and week-three, there were precisely seven years. Between week-sixty-eight and week-sixty-nine, there were precisely seven years. By what Scriptural authority was I to believe God ordained the unit of measure between the last two weeks to change from seven years to two thousand years? I challenge you to look again at the six things which were to be accomplished during the seventy weeks and their timing as declared in Daniel 9:24-25. I include these below for your review.

> 24"Seventy weeks are determined For your people and
> for your holy city, To finish the transgression, To make an
> end of sins, To make reconciliation for iniquity, To bring in
> everlasting righteousness, To seal up vision and proph-
> ecy, And to anoint the Most Holy. 25"Know therefore and

> understand, That from the going forth of the command To restore and build Jerusalem Until Messiah the Prince, There shall be seven weeks and sixty-two weeks; The street shall be built again, and the wall, Even in troublesome times. —Daniel 9:24-25

Notice that the Messiah does not come until sixty-nine of the seventy weeks are concluded. The ramifications of a two-thousand-year gap between week-sixty-nine and week-seventy become rather obvious. It means that the revealing of Israel's Messiah does not happen during the seventy-week prophecy but in between the sixty-ninth and seventieth-week. It also places the ministry, death, burial, and resurrection of Jesus Christ outside of the seventy-week prophecy. Since the six things that were to be accomplished per verse 24 did not happen in the first sixty-nine weeks, then they are yet to occur. Does that mean that a provision for sins, iniquities, and righteousness is yet to be accomplished? If so, by whom and when will it be performed? If you believe the Lord is the provider of these things and that they will happen after the interval, what proof-text do you cite? Even if you embrace a two-thousand-year interval, the seventieth week of Daniel will be finished before the Lord returns to the earth.

What About "The Time of Jacob's Trouble"?

The event referred to as "the time of Jacob's trouble" appears only one time in the Scriptures. Below I have listed that Scripture passage for your convenience.

> 3For behold, the days are coming,' says the LORD, 'that I will bring back from captivity My people Israel and Judah,' says the LORD. 'And I will cause them to return to the land that I gave to their fathers, and they shall possess it.'" 4Now these are the words that the Lord spoke concerning Israel and Judah. 5"For thus says the LORD: 'We have heard a voice of trembling, Of fear, and not of peace. 6Ask now, and see, Whether a man is ever in labor with child? So why do I see every man with his hands on his loins Like a woman in labor, And all faces turned pale? 7Alas! For that day is great, So that none is like it; And it is the time of Jacob's trouble, But he shall be saved out of it. 8'For it shall come to pass in that day,' Says the LORD of hosts, 'That I will break his yoke from your neck, And will burst your bonds; Foreigners shall no more enslave them. 9But they shall serve the LORD their God, And David their king, Whom I will raise up for them. 10'Therefore do not fear, O My servant Jacob,' says the LORD, 'Nor be dismayed, O Israel; For behold, I will save you from afar, And your seed from the land of their captivity. Jacob shall return, have rest and be quiet, And no one shall make him afraid. 11For I am with you,' says the LORD, 'to save you; Though I make a full end of all nations where I have scattered you, Yet I will not make a complete end of you. But I will correct you in justice, And will not let you go altogether unpunished.'
>
> —Jeremiah 30:3-11

"The time of Jacob's trouble" is referenced in the above passage in verse seven. The context of this passage clearly speaks of a prophecy that will find its fulfillment in the last days of this age.

Many cite "the time of Jacob's trouble" and "the great tribulation period" as being synonymous. Are these claims legitimate? First of all, it is essential to remember that Jacob's name was changed to Israel. This happened after his wrestling match with the Lord at Bethel as he was fleeing from the wrath of his brother, Esau. Jacob is the father of the twelve tribes of Israel. Therefore, Jacob's trouble speaks of a time of great difficulty prophesied concerning the nation of Israel.

In my previous book, *The Terminal Generation,* I built a case concerning the makeup of the last seven years of this age and how it would unfold according to the Scriptures. I showed you that the last seven years was divided up into two 3½ years segments. Though many contend that this seven-year period is the tribulation period, I believe only the first half of this period is to be considered as the tribulation period. The first 3½ years is the great tribulation period and the last 3½ years is the great day of God's wrath, commonly referred to as the Day of the Lord. The world's focus during the great tribulation will be the destruction of the Church. I believe the attention of the world during the last 3½ years will be on the destruction of the nation of Israel and the seizing of God's holy city, Jerusalem. I am convinced "Jacob's Trouble" will begin shortly after the conclusion of the tribulation period in the fifth seal and the announcement of the great day of God's wrath in the sixth seal. It will conclude at the second coming of the Lord with His saints to engage the armies of this world at the battle of Armageddon. At that time, Jesus, the King of kings, will set up His rule and reign over the whole world for one thousand years. During this time, God will restore Israel and Jerusalem and bless them above all the nations of the world. The verses following the above passage in Jeremiah, chapter thirty (verses 12-24) speak of this period commonly referred to as the millennial kingdom.

SECTION 3

The Feasts of the Lord

(Spiritual Journey of God's People)

CHAPTER 10

The Spring Feasts

Introduction

Before I begin to develop a timeline of what to expect during the last days of this age, I would like to lay a foundation by discussing the spring and fall feasts. You might ask, "What do these feasts have to do with an eschatological timeline?" It is essential to realize that these feasts were holy convocations God commanded Israel to observe annually. Their spiritual significance was very meaningful. The feasts celebrated each year were to be symbolic of the whole spiritual journey of God's people from the beginning of the age to its end. Each year God required that all male adults appear before Him three times. Those times were at Passover, which represented the three spring feasts, at Tabernacles which represented the three fall feasts, and also at Pentecost, the one feast in-between the spring and fall feasts. These seven feasts in total were to serve as a dress rehearsal of the ultimate prophetic fulfillment, which would one day come to pass through the ministry of Jesus Christ on this earth. Most of the major eschatological events that were prophesied will occur on one of the seven feasts Israel was commanded to observe annually.

Our goal is not an in-depth study of the feasts but rather a brief overview to give sufficient information to be able to see their eschatological significance. For a more detailed study, there are many excellent resources available, such as Kevin J. Conner's book, "The Feasts of Israel."

Let us begin our study by discussing the feasts that Christ fulfilled already during His first coming to this earth. We will start by looking at the Feast of Passover, which is the first holy convocation of the year Israel was to observe.

Passover

The first Passover happened in Egypt when God's people were to sacrifice an unblemished lamb, put the blood on the lintel and doorposts of each house, and eat it that night while fully dressed and ready to travel. When the angel of death went forth throughout all of Egypt that night, the firstborn of man and beast died, upon which the angel did not see the sacrificial blood. Israel was to celebrate this great deliverance out of Egyptian bondage as a memorial every year. However, it was to be more than a mere celebration. It represented a typological fulfillment of a future prophesied fulfillment that God promised would usher in eternal deliverance for His people. He would send His people a Passover lamb that would take away the sins of the world on the condition His blood would be applied to their lives by faith.

> [7]Therefore purge out the old leaven, that you may be a new lump since you truly are unleavened. For indeed Christ, our Passover, was sacrificed for us. [8]Therefore let us keep the feast, not with old leaven, nor with the leaven of malice and wickedness, but with the unleavened bread of sincerity and truth. —1 Corinthians 5:7-8

On the fourteenth day of Nissan, which is the first month of the sacred calendar, Israel was to annually re-enact this feast as a perpetual typological dress rehearsal until Jesus, our ultimate Passover, was sacrificed. This salvation experience begins that believer's spiritual journey.

> [4]"These are the feasts of the Lord, holy convocations which you shall proclaim at their appointed times. [5]On the fourteenth day of the first month at twilight is the Lord's Passover. —Leviticus 23:4-5

The three spring feasts occurred during the first month of Nissan, the three fall feasts happened during the seventh month of Tishri, and the feast between the feasts happened during the third month of Sivan. The sighting of the new moon for the month of Nissan was critical because the feasts were all determined and charted from the first day of Nissan. Their civil calendar consisted of twelve or thirteen months with its new year beginning with Tishri, which is also the seventh month of the sacred calendar.

It is incredible to me that at twilight on Nissan 14 in the year our Lord died, the Lamb of God was being sacrificed at the very same moment the annual Passover lamb was. Jesus fulfilled this feast on the exact day and time as was customary every year. Not only that, but He also met all of the requirements God commanded concerning this feast. For example, the Passover lamb was to be brought into the house on Nissan 10, which was four days before the sacrifice. During this time the lamb was to be inspected for any fault or blemish. Jesus made His triumphal entry into Jerusalem and was brought into the house of God on Nissan 10. Just like the Passover lamb, He was before the people to be observed, inspected, and finally on the day of preparation, before Passover, He was declared by Pontius Pilate to be without fault. As with the dress rehearsal, so it is with the actual fulfillment.

Feast of Unleavened Bread

On Nissan 15, the feast of unleavened bread was to begin and be observed for one week. The first and seventh days of that week were to be kept as a High Sabbaths.

> 6And on the fifteenth day of the same month is the Feast of Unleavened Bread to the Lord; seven days you must eat unleavened bread. 7On the first day you shall have a holy convocation; you shall do no customary work on it. 8But you shall offer an offering made by fire to the Lord for seven days. The seventh day shall be a holy convocation; you shall do no customary work on it.' "
>
> —Leviticus 23:6-8

Regardless of what day of the week the Passover fell, the following day was always a Sabbath. This is why they had to get the body of Jesus off the cross and in the tomb before sundown, which began the evening of Nissan15. In the year Jesus was crucified, Passover was on Wednesday. Yes, you heard me right. He died on Good Wednesday, not Good Friday. Let me explain.

Most people assume that because the day after Christ died was a Sabbath, He had to have been crucified on Friday. Do the math. How could Jesus die on Friday, spend three days and three nights in the grave, and the tomb be found empty by daybreak on Sunday? Let's look at the Scriptures to see what they say concerning this. Before doing this, let me make a point about how a day is defined in the Bible. We Gentiles count a day as beginning in the morning and ending in the evening. However, God says in Genesis that the evening and the morning was the first day. Like God, the Jews define a day as beginning with the evening at sunset and concluding the following day at sunset. And now, let us do the math.

The first day of the Feast of Unleavened Bread was a High Sabbath, and it officially began at sundown on Wednesday, which is the beginning of Thursday evening (1st night in the grave). It lasted until sunset on Thursday (1st day in the grave). Since Thursday was a Sabbath, the women could not buy spices to anoint the Lord's body until the following day.

> 1Now when the Sabbath was past, Mary Magdalene, Mary the mother of James, and Salome bought spices, that they might come and anoint Him. 2Very early in the

> morning, on the first day of the week, they came to the tomb when the sun had risen. —Mark 16:1-2

The High Sabbath ended that day at sunset which began Friday evening (2nd night in the grave). Friday during the day (2nd day in the grave) they were able to go purchase the anointing supplies. At sunset, of that same day, which is the beginning of Saturday evening (3rd night in the grave) the weekly Sabbath day began and lasted until sunset Saturday (3rd day in the grave). This meant that the women could not go anoint Jesus the day after they bought the spices, for it too was a Sabbath. Having spent three nights and three days in the grave, Jesus was raised from the dead shortly before sunset on Saturday. I know that most say He arose on the first day of the week, but the Scriptures declare His tomb was found empty at sunrise Sunday. For Him to raise after sunset on Saturday would have caused Him to spend part or all of a fourth night in the tomb. In the year of our Lord's crucifixion, the week had to contain two Sabbaths with one day separating them to satisfy the Scriptures.

> [1]Now on the first day of the week, very early in the morning, they, and certain other women with them, came to the tomb bringing the spices which they had prepared.
> [2]But they found the stone rolled away from the tomb.
> [3]Then they went in and did not find the body of the Lord Jesus. —Luke 24:1-3

The last two passages above prove that there was a Sabbath between the preparation of the spices and the women taking these to the tomb on the first day of the week (Sunday) to anoint the body of Jesus.

How does this feast relate to the spiritual journey of God's children? Whereas the emphasis of the Passover was to mark the beginning of the believer's spiritual journey, the Feast of Unleavened Bread was about getting the leaven or sin out of the life of the believer. During this feast, which lasted seven days, God's people were to thoroughly purge their house of all leaven and eat only unleavened bread. The significance of seven days is that "Seven" marks the time of completion or maturity. This was symbolic of the maturation process that takes place after one's birth, whether physical or spiritual.

Feast of Firstfruits

The high priest, after offering up the Passover lamb, was then to go into seclusion to remain ceremonially clean until the time of the appointed offering he was to wave before God. Before the beginning of the High Sabbath, those serving the high priest were to reap and deliver a firstfruit sheaf of barley to the high priest to be held until the time of the firstfruits wave offering. This sheaf was the first portion of the firstfruits of the barley harvest or the first of the first.

> 26"The first of the firstfruits of your land you shall bring to the house of the Lord your God. —Exodus 34:26

This was always to be waved on the morning after the weekly Sabbath following the sacrifice of the Passover lamb.

> 10"Speak to the children of Israel, and say to them: 'When you come into the land which I give to you, and reap

> its harvest, then you shall bring a sheaf of the firstfruits of your harvest to the priest. [11]He shall wave the sheaf before the Lord, to be accepted on your behalf; on the day after the Sabbath the priest shall wave it' "
>
> —Leviticus 23:10-11

As the Jewish high priest was in seclusion three days and three nights after the crucifixion, so also was Jesus, our High Priest, secluded in the heart of the earth for three days and three nights.

> [40]For as Jonah was three days and three nights in the belly of the great fish, so will the Son of Man be three days and three nights in the heart of the earth.
>
> —Matthew 12:40

On the year of the crucifixion, the women left early so they would arrive at the tomb by sunrise on Sunday morning. Finding the tomb empty, Mary lingered on after the others left. Weeping, she looked into the tomb and saw two angels who asked her why she was crying. Mary told them it was because someone had come and stolen the body of her Lord. Then she turned around and saw what she thought was the gardener and asked him if he knew where the Lord's body was. Jesus called her by name, and Mary then recognized it was the Lord. Before she could embrace Him, Jesus told her not to touch Him because He had not yet ascended to His Father.

> [13]Then they said to her, "Woman, why are you weeping?" She said to them, "Because they have taken away

> my Lord, and I do not know where they have laid Him."
> [14]Now when she had said this, she turned around and
> saw Jesus standing there, and did not know that it was
> Jesus. [15]Jesus said to her, "Woman, why are you weeping?
> Whom are you seeking?" She, supposing Him to be the
> gardener, said to Him, "Sir, if You have carried Him away,
> tell me where You have laid Him, and I will take Him
> away." [16]Jesus said to her, "Mary!" She turned and said to
> Him, "Rabboni!" (which is to say, Teacher). [17]Jesus said to
> her, "Do not cling to Me, for I have not yet ascended to
> My Father; but go to My brethren and say to them, 'I am
> ascending to My Father and your Father, and to My God
> and your God.'"
>
> —John 20:13-17

Why would Jesus say that? It was because our Passover Lamb had now become our High Priest who was about to wave the firstfruits offering before His Father. Remember, if the high priest touched anything common or unclean, he had to start the cleansing ritual again before waving the firstfruits offering to God. While the Jewish high priest was waving the firstfruits of the barley harvest to God, Jesus was also offering to His Father a sheaf of the firstfruits. This firstfruits harvest consisted of those who were the first to be reaped from the grave. These saints were raised from the grave the same day Jesus was resurrected.

> [52]and the graves were opened; and many bodies of the
> saints who had fallen asleep were raised; [53]and coming
> out of the graves after His resurrection, they went into
> the holy city and appeared to many.
>
> —Matthew 27:52-53

The wave offering being accomplished, Jesus then appeared to His disciples and told them they could now touch Him to prove He was not just a spirit.

> 9And as they went to tell His disciples, behold, Jesus met them, saying, "Rejoice!" So they came and held Him by the feet and worshiped Him. 10Then Jesus said to them, "Do not be afraid. Go and tell My brethren to go to Galilee, and there they will see Me." —Matthew 28:9-10

How does this feast relate to the spiritual journey of the people of God from the beginning to the end? It speaks of a firstfruits sampling before His coming of the final harvest of all who die in Christ at the rapture.

CHAPTER 11

THE FALL FEASTS

Introduction

During His first coming and before His ascension, Jesus fulfilled the three spring feasts on the very day and hour that the Jews were observing them according to God's instruction. I firmly believe He will be no less precise when fulfilling the three fall feasts. The lone feast separating the spring and fall feasts, we will discuss in Section 4. I am referring to the Feast of Weeks, also known as the Feast of Pentecost. This feast was fulfilled after His ascension and before His return. This happens in between His two earthly visits.

Before we consider the three fall feasts, I want to briefly share some basics about the Jewish calendar system. It is important to realize that Israel had two calendars they observed each year. The sacred calendar began at the sighting of the new moon which began the month of Nissan, which corresponds with March-April on the Gregorian calendar. The seven annual feasts that Israel was to keep as holy convocations were observed in the first seven months of the sacred calendar. The beginning of each month of the sacred and civil calendars was determined by the sighting of the new moon after the conclusion of the previous month. Two reliable watchmen were posted on the wall at Jerusalem to watch for the first sign of the new, crescent moon at sunset each month. These watchmen were referred to as the two witnesses. This was somewhat unpredictable and could not be determined by only counting. God would adjust the lunar calendar to sync up with the solar year by adding days and even an additional month from time to time. Even our calendar varies from month to month to adjust the lunar time to equal a solar year.

When the two witnesses sighted the new moon each month, they were to confirm the sighting by blowing a long shofar/trumpet blast to notify the people that the beginning of the new month was officially here. The celebration of "Rosh Chodesh" (new month) was to be sanctified by the people much like a Sabbath. The blowing of the trumpets was a signal for the people of God to stop their work, their daily routines, and assemble together at the temple to offer sacrifices, worship, and feast together. These festivities were observed monthly. With these facts in mind, let us now look at the fall feasts.

Feast of Trumpets

The Feast of Trumpets heralded the close of the harvest after the firstfruits offering at Pentecost. It was a time of repentance and reckoning with God. It was also a time of expectation for new beginnings. This feast was to be observed on the first day of Tishri, which is the seventh month on Israel's sacred calendar. It is interesting to note that this is the only feast of the seven which was to be observed on the first day of the month. This made this particular "Rosh Chodesh" special from all the others since it fell on this holy convocation. It is the Jewish holiday known as "Rosh Hashanah," which means the head or beginning of the new year on the civil calendar. Why is that important? Since the Feast of Trumpets takes place on the first day of the month, then it begins at the sighting of the new moon, when just a sliver of the moon appears at sunset in the night sky. Since this has to be confirmed by eyewitness sightings, the weather has to be clear enough to observe the new moon. It is understandable that, because of the varying weather conditions and God varying the number of days some months, this process was not an exact science. Because of this, no one knew exactly the day or hour that this feast would begin. Until the sighting of the new moon by the two witnesses, the first day of the month could not be established.

For this reason, the Feast of Trumpets has come to be known as the feast that no one knows the day or the hour. Jesus used this same idiom to describe His coming to judge those who dwell on the earth and rapture His saints to forever be with Him. The use of this idiom in the Scriptures is not meant to portray His coming as being elusive or vague but actually is used to give more clarity and specificity as to when He will come. Just as His fulfillment of the spring feasts happened on their specifically assigned days, so too will His coming be at the very same time as the Feast of

Trumpets. He is coming to fully redeem the purchased possession, which is His bride, the Church.

> [13]In Him you also trusted, after you heard the word of truth, the gospel of your salvation; in whom also, having believed, you were sealed with the Holy Spirit of promise, [14]who is the guarantee of our inheritance until the redemption of the purchased possession, to the praise of His glory. —Ephesians 1:13-14

Notice in verse 13 that the downpayment for the espoused bride was the outpouring of the Holy Spirit on the day of Pentecost. From that day forward Christ has been preparing a place for His bride-to-be in His Father's house while here on earth the Holy Spirit has been preparing His bride for the permanent union with her Husband-to-be.

"Rosh Hashanah" heralded the beginning of the period known as the High Holy Days with Yom Kippur (The Day of Atonement) occurring ten days later, on the tenth of Tishri. Those ten days are known as "The Days of Awe," a time of national repentance for Israel. It was a time of penitence, prayer, and fasting, in preparation for the Feast of Atonement and the Feast of Tabernacles.

The Ten Days of Penitence are seen as an opportunity to change and be changed. I believe the ultimate fulfillment of this will be when the Church is purged, made white, and matured during the three and a half years of the Great Tribulation. As we discussed in my previous book, the "Day of the Lord" or the "Great Day of God's Wrath" will follow immediately after the tribulation, when for three and a half additional years God will seal His saints while He is judging the wicked who dwell on the earth. Though God is using this time period to judge the wicked, He will also use it to train His church to subdue, take dominion, and rule over this earth. At the end of the second half of the final week of years of this age, and at the last trump, God will catch away all of His saints, both dead and alive. This event will conclude on earth the church's observance of the Feast of Trumpets.

Feast of Atonement

On the tenth day of the seventh month, the feast referred to as the Day of Atonement was to be observed. This was Israel's most solemn holy day since it dealt exclusively with atonement for the sin of the God's people.

> [27]"Also the tenth day of this seventh month shall be the Day of Atonement. It shall be a holy convocation for you; you shall afflict your souls, and offer an offering made by fire to the Lord. [32]It shall be to you a sabbath of solemn rest, and you shall afflict your souls; on the ninth day of the month at evening, from evening to evening, you shall celebrate your sabbath." —Leviticus 23:27,32

The people were to afflict their soul with fasting and prayer in preparation to stand trial before the heavenly court. At this time, God would review their lives of the past year and render a verdict. It was literally a court date where all Israel stood before their Judge. It was not only a day of cleansing, but also a time of exoneration of all iniquity, sin, transgression, and uncleanness. It was a pronouncement of innocence; it was a declaration of "not guilty." Only the high priest, as an advocate for the people of God, could go beyond the veil to sprinkle the blood of the atonement on the mercy seat within the Holy of Holies. The Hebrew name today for this feast is "Yom Kippur." The high priest would first bathe and then put on white linen undergarments and a white linen tunic and belt instead of his priestly ministry garments. By washing before entering the tent of meeting, the high priest avoided bringing any form of contamination into it. After having completed all the sacrifices and offerings he was commanded to do, the high priest went into the Holy of Holies, and the people awaited God's verdict. If the cloud descended into the Holy of Holies, causing the Shekinah glory to manifest to the high priest, the priest and the people rejoiced over the verdict of being forgiven and exonerated.

I believe this feast finds its ultimate fulfillment at the "Judgment Seat of Christ," also known as the "Bema Seat." The Greek word *Bema* means "the official seat of the Judge." Jesus, the High Priest of our profession, is our legal intermediary/lawyer. All of God's people must one day stand before the judgment seat of Christ to give an account of all the works we did as we walked this earth in our mortal bodies.

> 10But why do you judge your brother? Or why do you show contempt for your brother? For we shall all stand before the judgment seat of Christ. 11For it is written: "As I live, says the Lord, every knee shall bow to Me, and every tongue shall confess to God." 12So then each of us

> shall give an account of himself to God.
>
> —Romans 14:10-12

> [10]For we must all appear before the judgment seat of Christ, that each one may receive the things done in the body, according to what he has done, whether good or bad. —2 Corinthians 5:10

The timing of the judgment seat of Christ is at the last trumpet sound of the feast of trumpets, which is the seventh trump.

> [15]Then the seventh angel sounded: And there were
> loud voices in heaven, saying, "The kingdoms of this
> world have become the kingdoms of our Lord and of
> His Christ, and He shall reign forever and ever!" [18]The
> nations were angry, and Your wrath has come, and the
> time of the dead, that they should be judged, and that
> You should reward Your servants, the prophets and the
> saints, and those who fear Your name, small and great,
> and should destroy those who destroy the earth."
>
> —Revelation 11:15,18

I personally believe that in the year the saints of God are raptured, it will be a Jubilee, a time of true liberty, the likes of which has never been encountered before. On the tenth day of the "Ten Days of Awe" the shofar/trumpet of Jubilee, which marks the "Day of Atonement," will be sounded.

> [9]Then you shall cause the trumpet of the Jubilee to sound on the tenth day of the seventh month; on the

> Day of Atonement, you shall make the trumpet to sound throughout all your land. —Leviticus 25:9

Feast of Tabernacles

The Feast of Tabernacles is the seventh and last feast of the sacred calendar. It was observed in the seventh month of the sacred calendar, which is also the first month of the civil calendar.

God's people were to make portable tabernacles/shelters and dwell in them for seven days to remind them that after their deliverance from Egypt their dwelling places and the tabernacle of God were portable and temporary until they received their inheritance.

The institution of this feast can be seen in Leviticus 23.

> [33]Then the Lord spoke to Moses, saying, [34]"Speak to the children of Israel, saying: 'The fifteenth day of this seventh month shall be the Feast of Tabernacles for seven days to the Lord. [35]On the first day there shall be a holy convocation. You shall do no customary work on it. [36]For seven days you shall offer an offering made by fire to the Lord. On the eighth day you shall have a holy convocation, and you shall offer an offering made by fire to the Lord. It is a sacred assembly, and you shall do no customary work on it. —Leviticus 23:33-36

The start of this feast is five days after the ingathering of the final harvest. The antitype of this is clear. Immediately after the great harvest, the rapture, then the Feast of

Tabernacles began shortly after that. This speaks of the millennial kingdom, which is the seventh day or day of rest. It was to be celebrated for seven days, and on the eighth day, there should be a day of rest. The seventh day or seventh thousand-year period is followed by a time of "all things new," as the number eight is the number of new beginnings. I believe this is about the eternal state after the Great White Throne Judgment where there will be a new heaven and new earth. A time of new beginnings! Zechariah clearly prophesied the fact that at Christ's second coming when He comes to earth with His saints, those who are still alive and enter into the millennial kingdom will be required to celebrate the Feast of Tabernacles annually.

Remember, from Adam to the sacrifice of the Passover Lamb, Jesus, was a four day (four thousand years) inspection time. God then offered the church the priesthood as He did Israel. The Lord promised to be their God, and they would be His people. He promised them that He would come and tabernacle/meet with them after the two days of cleansing themselves before the meeting. From Adam to the millennial kingdom totals six thousand years, which is the number of man and labor. The union with God ushers in the seventh day or thousand-year period, which will be the age of rest. This happens during the millennial reign of Christ Jesus.

The Antitype

As a type, the feast of Tabernacles looks forward to the millennium when God comes to the earth to tabernacle with man. During this time, the people of God will have a long-awaited period of peace and rest. In fact, the prophet Zechariah made it clear that the feast of booths will be celebrated throughout the entirety of the millennium.

> 16And it shall come to pass that everyone who is left of all the nations which came against Jerusalem shall go up from year to year to worship the King, the Lord of hosts, and to keep the Feast of Tabernacles. 17And it shall be that whichever of the families of the earth do not come up to Jerusalem to worship the King, the Lord of hosts, on them there will be no rain. 18If the family of Egypt will not come up and enter in, they shall have no rain; they shall receive the plague with which the Lord strikes the nations who do not come up to keep the Feast of Tabernacles. 19This shall be the punishment of Egypt and the punishment of all the nations that do not come up to keep the Feast of Tabernacles.
>
> —Zechariah 14:16-19

In this section, we have covered the spring and fall feasts, which comprise six of the seven feasts of Israel. The lone feast that we did not include, the Feast of Pentecost, we will discuss in the next section of this book. I refer to this feast as the "feast between the feasts" because it occurred between the spring and fall feasts.

SECTION 4

From Now to Eternity

(A Prophetic Timeline)

CHAPTER 12

THE THIRD SEAL

Introduction to Timeline

I now want to paint a picture of a timeline from "Now to Eternity." I want to project a scenario of how it might play out beginning with these present days in 2019 until the ushering in of the eternal state, when time will no longer exist. I personally believe that we are currently in the midst of the third seal of Revelation, chapter six. I also believe we are fast moving toward its fulfillment and toward the opening of the fourth seal. I have included, for your convenience, a timeline in Appendix B of this book that spans a time-period from the cross to eternity.

What is the Third Seal?

As discussed in the book, *The Terminal Generation*, we showed you that the third seal represents inflation, not famine – Revelation 6:5-6.

> [5]When He opened the third seal, I heard the third living creature say, "Come and see." So I looked, and behold, a black horse, and he who sat on it had a pair of scales in his hand. [6]And I heard a voice in the midst of the four living creatures saying, "A quart of wheat for a denarius, and three quarts of barley for a denarius; and do not harm the oil and the wine." —Revelation 6:5-6

Notice that this passage does not say that food is scarce, but instead it is costly – a day's wages just to eat. In famine, food is not available at any cost. Before I continue, I ask for your patience as I build a basis for the point I will be endeavoring to make about inflation and its relevance to you and me in these last days.

First of all, let me share with you how the competition between nations and kingdoms, as referred to in the third sign of the Olivet Discourse, causes the phenomenon of inflation. Inflation is the direct result of governmental principalities who direct the affairs and agendas of earthly nations. Governments are the immediate results of spiritual principalities that have received authority and power to rule over the governments of the earth. These use their spiritual superiority to influence those over which they have been given dominion. These spiritual principalities are either a part of the kingdom of God or the kingdom of darkness. They are able to influence through revelation, knowledge, and supernatural encounter. These spiritual beings often offer supernatural power in exchange for a covenantal agreement between them and the receiving earthly recipients, to promote their agenda and spiritual principles. In Daniel's case, both kingdoms were trying to influence Daniel's world. Even though Daniel was seeking direction from the kingdom of light, a spiritual principality of the kingdom of darkness was resisting the spiritual principality sent by God, which was Gabriel, the prince. The spiritual principality that was opposing Gabriel was the prince of Persia, who was commissioned by Satan to rise up against and hinder the kingdom of God.

The devil's agenda has been the same since he was cursed in the garden. He was told that there would be enmity between his seed and the woman's seed and that the woman's seed was going to crush his head. Since that time he has been on a mission to corrupt that seed and render it ineffective against him. His first attempt at this agenda was spoiled by the judgment of the flood in Noah's day. All that Satan had accomplished was wiped out, and God reinitiated His plan afresh with eight people who were righteous. Once again the devil tried to pollute the whole world by rallying them around his agenda and government to overthrow God's. He had so unified the people at the tower of Babel that God felt it necessary to come down and once again disrupt the plan the devil was implementing, through a governmental proxy by the name of Nimrod.

As you know, God caused disunity among them by confusing their language and ultimately their ability to communicate and work together. However, the story does not end there. Ever since Babel, the devil has been working feverishly to once again "re-babel-ize" the world. This explains all the chatter we are currently hearing about a new world order composed of a one world government, a one world financial system, and a one world currency all dedicated to fulfilling a one world agenda under the direction of the kingdom of darkness. As before, God will come down to earth in judgment and foil Satan's plan at the battle of Armageddon. If that was not enough, the Bible prophesies that even at the end of the millennial kingdom the devil will make a final attempt to accomplish the very same agenda. He will do this when he is loosed from his chains in the bottomless pit at the end of the thousand-year rule and reign of Christ and His saints. I am sharing all of this with you to demonstrate the fact that competition between kingdoms and nations result in negative consequences of which inflation poses one of the gravest effects.

Now let us define inflation. Most people define inflation through a government-pushed narrative that obscures what is really happening. Governments, and the economists under them, define inflation as a rise in the prices of commodities at a substantial rate over a considerable period of time, thus requiring more money to buy a given amount of goods and services. This narrative convinces people that inflation is the result of pressures in the market and the law of supply and demand. This is what your government wants you to think so we don't catch on as to what the real culprit behind inflation is. Let's look at how Webster's dictionary defines inflation: "inflation is the increase in the amount of currency in circulation, resulting in a relatively sharp and sudden fall in its value and a rise in prices." Wow! That sure exposes the narrative we have been fed and by which we have been misled.

How does the increase in the amount of money in circulation happen? It occurs when governments print more money to be able to pay the debts because of their out-of-control spending addiction. If we as citizens print money as a solution to our overspending, we go to jail. Why is it then legal for governments to do this? Every unearned $100 bill that is spent into circulation devalues the earned $100 bill. If the government printed and put into circulation an extra $50 for every $100 earned, this would cause our $100 bill to be worth just $0.67. This shows what inflation really is – a hidden tax. Printing money with no substantive, value-based standard is just code for raising taxes. Tax has always been the scourge and agenda of earthly governments. Let me explain.

Let's look at a hypothetical yet practical example that gives a more precise understanding of what inflation really is and its actual cause. Let's say a twenty-two-year-old college graduate was given $10,000 by his parents to begin his new career. His new job pays him $100,000 per year, of which he puts $10,000 per year into his savings. If the rate of inflation is a moderate 5 percent, the following describes how inflation affects his financial value over time. After working for two years, the $10,000 gift from his parents is now worth only $9,000, and his second year $100,000 salary will now be worth only $95,000. After twenty years, the $10,000 gift will be worth $3,600 and his $100,000 salary, should he not get a raise in that period, will have a purchasing power of $36,000.

The governments of this world are controlling the narrative so the people won't get wise to the insidious agenda influenced by the financial elite of this world to destroy the economies of the individual nations. Its end goal is making it absolutely essential to establish a unified new world order with all of its trimmings. This plays into the devil's agenda of re-babel-izing the world to revolt against God and His people.

I personally believe this seal depicting hyperinflation is where we currently are with respect to God's prophetic timeline. The elitist agenda is methodically bringing our world into the fullness of this third seal at such a pace that it will soon be our world's present reality.

CHAPTER 13

The Fourth Seal

What is the Fourth Seal?

It is interesting to note that the first four of the seven seals speaks of a horse of a specific color going forth into the earth. The four horses and their respective riders go forth on the earth with a particular agenda and mission to accomplish. These riders were not on foot, but on horses, which is an indication that the effects of their presence will be felt more swiftly on the earth. Each of these seals not only describes the color of the horse but also the one who is riding the horse. Like the third seal we just finished discussing, the fourth seal involves the activities and influences of supernatural entities affecting the natural course of life on the earth in a very negative way. This is also true about the first two seals. In the first seal, it is the spirit of Antichrist going forth to deceive. In the second seal, it is a spiritual being that has the power to take peace from the earth and its inhabitants.

With this in mind, let us take a closer look at the fourth seal which is found in Revelation 6:7-8.

> [7]When He opened the fourth seal, I heard the voice of the fourth living creature saying, "Come and see." [8]So I looked, and behold, a pale horse. And the name of him who sat on it was Death, and Hades followed with him. And power was given to them over a fourth of the earth, to kill with sword, with hunger, with death, and by the beasts of the earth. —Revelation 6:7-8

Though the first three seals describe the riders that sit upon their different colored horses, the fourth seal reveals the name of its rider. The name of the spiritual being that is riding the pale-colored horse is "Death," who is the spirit of death. The Greek word for death, *tha'natos*, means "a separating of the soul from the body which ends life on this earth." It often implies the idea of future misery in a region enveloped with thick darkness. This rider's agenda will be to kill a fourth of the inhabitants of the earth. His mission is to accomplish this through four severe types of judgment. This seal also mentions another rider who goes forth with Death. His name is Hades which is the name of the god of the lower regions. According to Strong's, in Biblical Greek, Hades is associated with Orcus, the infernal regions in the very depths of the earth which serve as a receptacle of disembodied spirits. Some argue that the Hades that followed Death in this passage is about a spiritual place, not the name of a spiritual being. However, as you examine the sentence following the words Death and Hades, you will notice that it says, "And power was given 'them' over a fourth of the earth to kill..." The word "them" would indicate more than one being had the power to kill.

CHAPTER 13: THE FOURTH SEAL

Now let us speak more specifically about the four severe types of judgment that will claim the lives of one-fourth of the earth's population. Though various biblical translations use different words in verse 8 to describe these judgments, they all mean the same thing. For your convenience, I have listed below this verse in both the NKJV and ESV translations of Revelation 6:8b:

> 8And power was given to them over a fourth of the earth, to kill with sword, with hunger, with death, and by the beasts of the earth. —Revelation 6:8 (NKJV)

> 8And they were given authority over a fourth of the earth, to kill with sword and with famine and with pestilence and by wild beasts of the earth.
> —Revelation 6:8 (ESV)

The first judgment is the sword. In Greek, this word means "a long sword or javelin." According to Strong's, it can refer to any weapon of the kind. I believe this judgment is not war, as that would be a repeat of the second seal. I am convinced this refers to murder as a reaction to the various spiritual, social, political, and economic conditions prevalent in society. The second judgment, famine, would lend itself to this conclusion. If there is a worldwide famine, people will kill for food and the essentials of life. Not only would starvation explain a lot of this behavior but so would adverse spiritual, social, and political conditions/influences, leading to such action as hatred, murder, anarchy, racism, occultism, discrimination against various religious ideologies, and persecution. The third judgment is death (NKJV) or pestilence (ESV). The Greek word is *tha'natos*, which is the same word used as the name of the rider sitting on the pale horse. This Greek word can also mean "pestilence" according to Strong's. It makes sense that where the death of humans and beasts is prevalent because of the adverse earthly conditions, there would be pestilence following closely. Some translations translate *death* as "plagues." This could include both known and unknown diseases, viruses, and infections resulting from the natural and spiritual environmental conditions of the earth. The fourth judgment is the wild beasts of the earth. Desperate starving animals might add humans to their food chain whereas before they would not. And let us not forget that in Noah's day there were hybrid beings as a result of spiritual beings mixing their seed with the seed of man - see Genesis 6:4-5 and Daniel 2:42-43. With all the experimentations with the genomes of humans and animals that are happening, I wouldn't rule out any possibilities that men have imagined or have yet to imagine.

When we compare these judgments with those listed in Leviticus, Jeremiah, and Ezekiel, one cannot help but wonder if these things that were prophesied over Israel if they did wickedly are not the same judgments being spoken of in this passage. If God so judged the people He chose out of all the nations of the earth, why would we think it strange that He would do the same to the nations, or even to His church? Notice the very same judgments are spoken of in Ezekiel 5:17.

> [17]I will send famine and wild beasts against you, and they will rob you of your children. Pestilence and blood shall pass through you, and I will bring the sword upon you. I am the LORD; I have spoken." —Ezekiel 5:17

It is sobering to think that all of this death is going to take place prior to the great tribulation. Imagine the trembling and shaking that will take place when one out of every four people on the earth die. Could this be the great shaking alluded to in Hebrew 12:25-29?

> [25]See that you do not refuse Him who speaks. For if they did not escape who refused Him who spoke on earth, much more shall we not escape if we turn away from Him who speaks from heaven, [26]whose voice then shook the earth; but now He has promised, saying, "Yet once more I shake not only the earth but also heaven." [27]Now this, "Yet once more," indicates the removal of those things that are being shaken, as of things that are made, that the things which cannot be shaken may remain. [28]Therefore, since we are receiving a kingdom which cannot be shaken, let us have grace, by which we may serve God acceptably with reverence and godly fear. [29]For our God is a consuming fire.
>
> —Hebrews 12:25-29

Notice that the purpose of this great shaking is to make manifest what or who cannot be moved by the shaking. This is kind of reminiscent of what Psalm 91 speaks of when it says, though a thousand shall fall at your side and ten thousand at your right hand, it shall not come near you. I believe that when this shaking does occur, the only way to walk successfully is by walking in the Spirit and on the highway of holiness as declared in the Scripture below.

> 8A highway shall be there, and a road and it shall be called the Highway of Holiness. The unclean shall not pass over it, but it shall be for others. Whoever walks the road, although a fool, shall not go astray. 9No lion shall be there, nor shall any ravenous beast go up on it; it shall not be found there. But the redeemed shall walk there, 10And the ransomed of the Lord shall return, and come to Zion with singing, with everlasting joy on their heads. They shall obtain joy and gladness, and sorrow and sighing shall flee away. —Isaiah 35:8-10

CHAPTER 14

Psalm 83 War

Introduction

Some interesting questions are often raised concerning the war described in Psalm 83. Some of the questions being asked are: "Has it already happened?" or "Is it yet to happen?" If it has already happened, "When did it happen historically?" If it is yet to happen, "Is it the same war as the battle of Gog and Magog as described in Ezekiel chapters 38 and 39?" If these are two distinctly different wars, "In what order do they occur?" And finally, "When does each one occur in relation to the tribulation period?" These are some of the questions that have scholars scouring Scriptures in search of answers. Let's deal with the Psalm 83 war first. There are several views concerning the interpretation of Psalm 83.

Some believe this prophecy has already been fulfilled. Of those who do, most think it was fulfilled during the six-day war of 1967 when a confederacy of nations surrounding Israel went to war against her. The countries of Egypt, Lebanon, Syria, Jordan, and Iraq, along with displaced Palestinians, were a part of this confederacy. Though being outnumbered, total population wise, by more than twenty-eight to one, Israel had these nations begging for mercy in just six days of fighting. Despite the overwhelming odds, God's providential workings gave Israel a decisive victory over this Arab confederacy.

Others believe that this prophecy is yet to be fulfilled. Of these, some think that the Psalm 83 war is the same as the war of Gog and Magog, while others believe that these are two distinctly separate wars. Those who have this viewpoint in common find themselves disagreeing about the order in which they happen and when they occur concerning the tribulation period. Now let us examine Psalm 83 to see if we can discover some answers to questions cited above.

The Context of Psalm 83

The context of this Psalm is a prophetic prayer asking God to not be silent and still any longer but get involved because of what is happening to Israel at the time to which this prophecy was pointing.

> 1A Song. A Psalm of Asaph. Do not keep silent, O God!
> Do not hold Your peace, And do not be still, O God!
> 2For behold, Your enemies make a tumult; And those
> who hate You have lifted up their head. 3They have
> taken crafty counsel against Your people and consulted
> together against Your sheltered ones. 4They have said,
> "Come, and let us cut them off from being a nation, That
> the name of Israel may be remembered no more." 5For

> they have consulted together with one consent; They form a confederacy against You. [6]The tents of Edom and the Ishmaelites; Moab and the Hagrites; [7]Gebal, Ammon, and Amalek; Philistia with the inhabitants of Tyre; [8]Assyria also has joined with them; They have helped the children of Lot. Selah —Psalm 83:1-8

Note they remind God that His enemies, who hate Him, are the problem. They are stirring up trouble and raising their head against Him by taking counsel to come against His people, Israel. They proceed to inform God what the enemy's crafty counsel and the ultimate goal was. They intended to cut Israel off from being a nation and cause her name to be remembered no more. They also tell God that the countries surrounding them have formed a confederacy against Israel, that their counsel and goal might become a reality.

At this point in the Psalm, one cannot tell the time period to which this prophecy is referring. Throughout Israel's history, the nations have conspired against her. This, no doubt, is because the devil has always hated and spitefully come against those who God loves. Let us continue to examine this Psalm to see if there are any clues to determine whether or not this has or has not happened.

Has Psalm 83 Been Fulfilled?

In verse 6, the nations and people groups making up this confederacy are identified.

> [6]tents of Edom and the Ishmaelites; Moab and the Hagrites; [7]Gebal, Ammon, and Amalek; Philistia with the

> inhabitants of Tyre; [8]Assyria also has joined with them; They have helped the children of Lot. Selah
>
> —Psalm 83:6-8

The nations represented by these people are as follows: Edom, Moab, and Ammon dwelt in various regions of what is now known as Jordan. The Ishmaelites lived in Saudi Arabia and part of southern Jordan. The Hagrites refers to people in Egypt. The inhabitants of Tyre and Gebal dwelt in Lebanon. Philistia refers to the Gaza Strip. Assyria refers to a part of the nation of Syria and possibly northern Iraq. Amalek refers to the Arabs that live south of Israel, which would include the Sinai Peninsula and parts of Saudi Arabia. The children of Lot have already been mentioned as dwelling in Jordan, since Abraham's brother, Haran, was the father of Lot whose two sons were Moab and Ammon.

At this time, I would like to draw your attention to the people groups of this confederacy that settled in some of these nations. Verse six speaks of the "tents of Edom and the Ishmaelites." People living in tents instead of houses and cities carry the connotation of being wandering nomads separated from civilized society. Both of these groups were displaced refugees. Let me explain. Though both of the fathers of Ishmael and Edom (Esau) were a part of the genealogy of Christ, these sons were not. They were castaways, or refugees, from the commonwealth of Christ. They each settled in regions of the nations of this confederacy. The Ishmaelites primarily settled in Saudi Arabia. The Edomites settled in the mountains surrounding Mt. Seir in southern Jordan.

Remember the story of Jacob and Esau? Esau and Jacob were twins. When their father, Isaac, was about to die, Jacob by deceit stole the birthright of his first-born brother, Esau. He had to flee for his life, and there has been bad blood between the two ever since. Genesis records some interesting facts about Esau. It says that after eating the red soup of Jacob, his name was called Edom, which means "red." Genesis 36:1, when recording the genealogy of Esau, says that Esau is Edom. Even as the generations of Jacob were renamed Israel, so Esau's generations have been renamed Edom, who are the current day Palestinians. To this very day, there is animus between the lineage of Esau, the Palestinians, and the lineage of Jacob, the Israelites. From this, we can see that the confederacy spoken of in this passage consists of Jordan, Syria, Lebanon, Saudi Arabia, Egypt, the Gaza Strip, and Palestinian refugees. Though these refugees are scattered throughout many of these nations, their largest concentration is found in Jordan.

Let's compare this confederacy with that which fought against Israel in the six-day war in June of 1967. The five belligerents were Egypt, Syria, Jordan, Lebanon, and Iraq. Notice that the confederacy of Psalm 83 and the confederacy of the six-day war are different, even though some of the nations are participants in both. Iraq was a part of the six-day war but is not listed in the confederacy of the Psalm 83 war. Participants of the Psalm 83 war who were not a part of the six-day war include Saudi Arabia and the Gaza Strip. As a matter of fact, Saudi Arabia did not even offer support to the coalition of the six-day war. Therefore we conclude that the six-day war was not a prophetic fulfillment of Psalm 83. Because there is no historical evidence that such a confederacy has ever gone to war with Israel, we can also conclude that this war is yet to happen.

Is Psalm 83, Gog and Magog?

Now the question becomes, "Is the Psalm 83 war and the battle of Gog and Magog referring to the same war?" To answer this question, let us compare the confederacies listed in both. The confederacy of Gog and Magog can be found in Ezekiel chapter 38. We will look at this passage of Scripture in more detail in the next chapter. For now, let me list the nations that appear in the first six verses of Ezekiel 38. Russia, parts of the former USSR, and Iran (Persia) are the major players. Other nations that comprise this coalition include Cush (Sudan and Ethiopia), Put (Libya, Algeria, and Tunisia), Turkey and surrounding regions, and possibly Germany (Gomer). These two confederacies are not even close to being the same. This leads me to believe that these are two distinctly different wars. So now, we will set our focus on the Psalm 83 war.

The Psalm 83 War

Not one of the nations in this confederacy is listed as being a part of the coalition of Gog and Magog. When you consider the longstanding hate and vitriol of the people in the nations that geographically surround Israel, it confounds all logical thinking as to why they wouldn't gladly participate in this Russian/Iranian-led war. It begs the question, "Why would none of these nations gladly jump at the opportunity to see the destruction of Israel become a reality?" Could it be they had a change of heart toward Israel? I seriously doubt that. I personally believe the only two reasonable explanations could be as follows:

- Iran and/or Russia already absorbed them before the Psalm 83 war.

- The Arab confederacy described in Psalm 83 has already attempted such an assault on Israel and were soundly and entirely defeated. They were completely annexed, occupied, and governed by Israel.

My personal conviction is that it is the latter of the above options. This certainly would explain the absence of these nations in the Russian/Iranian coalition. If either or both of these scenarios are true, then the Psalm 83 war happens before the battle of Gog and Magog. Are there any Scriptures that would lend credence to such a notion?

I believe the prophet, Ezekiel, prophesied such a notion. The battle of Gog and Magog is recorded in Ezekiel chapters 38 and 39. Many of the preceding chapters predict the judgment of God upon the nations represented in Psalm 83 for their mistreatment of Israel. It also speaks of the judgment on Israel for departing from their God. Much of the context of these chapters deals with the conquests of King Nebuchadnezzar of Babylon and the punishments inflicted on these nations as a result of being defeated by his armies.

I am persuaded these judgments were a typological fulfillment of that which will ultimately come again near the end of the age. According to Ezekiel, when Israel was conquered and led away captive, the surrounding nations clapped their hands and rejoiced over Israel's demise. They even supported and assisted Nebuchadnezzar's invasion and triumph. Because of their celebration, God used Babylon to judge them also. Nothing has changed. Even today, these same neighboring nations perpetrate many evil acts against Israel and then celebrate her demise. What motivated God to judge them in the days of Nebuchadnezzar will cause Him to do so once again in the future. We will cover this in more detail later in this chapter.

Consequently, to limit these judgments to the time of Israel's Babylonian captivity only, I feel would be a theological miscue. Remember, Israel was led away captive again in 70 AD, and her demise was followed with the same response by their hateful surrounding neighbors. Often prophecy has a typological and ultimate fulfillment, and I believe this is the case in Ezekiel's prophecy. Though Nebuchadnezzar's name and exploits are mentioned frequently in the chapters leading up to Gog and Magog in chapter 38, the prophet jumps ahead from that time to the days in which we are currently living.

> [24]"And there shall no longer be a pricking brier or a painful thorn for the house of Israel from among all who are around them, who despise them. Then they shall know that I am the Lord GOD." [25]'Thus says the Lord GOD: "When I have gathered the house of Israel from the peoples among whom they are scattered, and am

> hallowed in them in the sight of the Gentiles, then they will dwell in their own land which I gave to My servant Jacob. 26And they will dwell safely there, build houses, and plant vineyards; yes, they will dwell securely, when I execute judgments on all those around them who despise them. Then they shall know that I am the LORD their God."' " —Ezekiel 28:24-26

The phrase, "When I have gathered the house of Israel from the peoples among whom they are scattered," speaks of Israel's repatriation to her land in 1948. This not only identifies a period long after Nebuchadnezzar's day but also supports the notion of the Babylonian captivity being typological of the ultimate fulfillment at the end of this age. Notice in verses 24-25 that something happens that removes the continual harassment by Israel's surrounding neighbors. I don't, for one minute, believe the bullying stops because of a change of her neighbors' attitudes and dispositions. Why then? The simple answer is the Psalm 83 war. God said this would happen after Israel is regathered, after God is sanctified in Israel in the sight of her neighbors, and after God brings His judgments on her neighbors. I believe this passage is referring to the Psalm 83 war when God's favor for Israel will be clearly seen by her enemies in their defeat. Now let us look at this war and how it might possibly unfold very soon.

What Will Happen In This War?

Some scholars contend that God alone executes the judgments on Israel's neighbors, and He does this during the "Day of the Lord" at His second coming. This means Israel has to contend with her enemies and wait to dwell securely and safely in her borders until the beginning of the millennial kingdom. I don't believe that at all. First of all, the "Day of the Lord" is not a single day and event, but rather a three and a half-year period beginning after the announcement of this day of wrath in the sixth seal and ending after the seventh seal and the second coming of Christ with His saints. We will cover this event and timing in more detail later in this book. Now as to the contention that God will bring judgments on Israel's neighbors without human involvement, let us look at a couple of passages of Scripture that deal with the judgments of Israel's neighbors. The first one is found in Ezekiel 25.

> [13]...therefore thus says the Lord GOD: "I will also stretch out My hand against Edom, cut off man and beast from it, and make it desolate from Teman; Dedan shall fall by the sword. [14]I will lay My vengeance on Edom by the hand of My people Israel, that they may do in Edom according to My anger and according to My fury; and they shall know My vengeance," says the Lord GOD.
>
> —Ezekiel 25:13-14

Notice in verse 14 that God said He would bring His vengeance on Edom by the hand of His people Israel. Yes, God is delivering the judgment, but to assume this means He will not use mankind to bring it to pass is a mistaken assumption. It is evident in verse 14 Israel represented God's anger and fury so that His enemies might know the vengeance of God. There are many examples of this in the Bible.

For instance, God judged Israel, but He used Assyria as His rod to do so. This being said, God at times does bring judgment without human involvement, as was the case with the destruction of Sodom and Gomorrah. The second passage is found in Numbers 24, which speaks about Jesus judging Moab and Edom, who both dwelt in the nation we now call Jordan.

> 17"I see Him, but not now; I behold Him, but not near; A Star shall come out of Jacob; A Scepter shall rise out of Israel, And batter the brow of Moab, And destroy all the sons of tumult 18"And Edom shall be a possession; Seir also, his enemies, shall be a possession, While Israel does valiantly. —Numbers 24:17-18

Notice that it says God will judge Moab and Edom but not by Himself. It will be while Israel does valiantly. Also, notice that not only does Israel defeat these enemies in this war but also takes possession of their lands. This is on the way to expanding her borders to match that which God prophesied over Abraham and his descendants as their inheritance.

> 18On the same day, the LORD made a covenant with Abram, saying: "To your descendants, I have given this land, from the river of Egypt to the great river, the River Euphrates— 19the Kenites, the Kenezzites, the Kadmonites, 20the Hittites, the Perizzites, the Rephaim, 21the Amorites, the Canaanites, the Girgashites, and the Jebusites." —Genesis 15:18-21

For a visual, there are many maps on the Internet showing the borders of the land mass God promised Abraham's descendants (see map in Appendix A). For now, I will attempt to describe it with words. Imagine the western boundary being the Nile River in Egypt. Follow the Nile to the southern border of Egypt. Then draw a line from there across the Red Sea passing through the middle of Saudi Arabia and Kuwait to where the Euphrates River empties into the Persian Gulf (at the border of Iraq and Kuwait). From there follow the Euphrates River northwest to Turkey and West to the Mediterranean Sea. When you are done, realize that you have just partitioned off a land mass that includes Egypt to the Nile River, the Sinai Peninsula, the Gaza Strip, Lebanon, Jordan, the Northwest half of Saudi Arabia, Kuwait, Iraq, Syria and, of course, modern-day Israel. I personally believe that the war described in Psalm 83 will reset the very borders God promised in making His covenant with Abraham. If not then, when in the remainder of this age could this possibly happen? Imagine the stir that would create in the watching world and the United Nations security council. History records that the UN struggled with the land mass seized by Israel in the six-day war and forced her to give much of it back. In that war, Israel captured the Sinai Peninsula and Gaza Strip from Egypt, the West Bank, and east Jerusalem from Jordan, and the Golan Heights from Syria. That pales in comparison with what God promised Abraham. There is a considerable discrepancy between the conquered land mass of the six-day war and the land mass Israel will acquire that belongs to the confederacy of Psalm 83. This should prove the six-day war is not the war of Psalm 83. As impossible as all this may seem, it is essential to remember that when God makes a covenantal promise, it will come to pass. As illogical and preposterous as it may seem, those who are God's must dare to believe this will happen and begin praying in faith for its fulfillment.

In summarizing the Psalm 83 war, Israel is going to, by the providence of God, rid herself of all her contentious and abusive neighbors in the same way Israel did throughout her wilderness journeys and biblical history as a nation. Psalm 83 lists examples of kings that troubled Israel in the past and how God judged them by the hand of His chosen people. The prophetic prayer in this Psalm asks God to do the same with the nations of this confederacy as He did in their past.

What will happen in the war is somewhat straightforward if you believe God has heard and will answer the prayer of Psalm 83. How all this will transpire is another matter of considerable speculation. I sincerely believe there are plenty of Scriptures related to this Psalm that give valuable insights as to "what will happen" as well as presenting logical possibilities as to "how it will happen." Allow me the grace to begin to speculate as to how this war might unfold by using the Scriptures. I in no way want to appear dogmatic but merely offer a possible scenario based on my understanding of biblical passages that address this subject matter.

CHAPTER 15

Psalm 83 War

(continued)

How Will This War Unfold?

The first passage I want to look at was spoken by the prophet, Obadiah, which has only one chapter. Verses 1-2 identify Edom as a people group that God will one day bring under judgment. Remember Edom and Esau are two names used to identify the Palestinians who are dispersed in several nations but primarily in Jordan. The prophet declares that God will make them small amongst the nations and much despised.

> 1The vision of Obadiah. Thus says the Lord GOD concerning Edom (We have heard a report from the LORD, And a messenger has been sent among the nations, saying, "Arise and let us rise up against her for battle"):
> 2"Behold, I will make you small among the nations; You shall be greatly despised. —Obadiah 1:1-2

In verses 6-9, God shares how they were led to their destruction.

> [6]"Oh, how Esau shall be searched out! How his hidden treasures shall be sought after! [7]All the men in your confederacy Shall force you to the border; The men at peace with you Shall deceive you and prevail against you. Those who eat your bread shall lay a trap for you. No one is aware of it. [8]"Will I not in that day," says the LORD, "Even destroy the wise men from Edom And understanding from the mountains of Esau? [9]Then your mighty men, O Teman, shall be dismayed, To the end that everyone from the mountains of Esau Maybe cut off by slaughter. —Obadiah 1:6-9

It is interesting to note that the Hebrew word, *beriyth*, that appears in verse 7 as a confederacy (alliance) is the same word used for the confederacy in Psalm 83:5. I believe these two passages are speaking of the same confederacy and their judgment. This confederacy will deceive, lay a trap, and force these Jordanian Palestinians out of the mountains to the border to be slaughtered by the Israeli army.

In verses 10-16, God gives precise details as to why He is going to judge Esau.

> [10]"For violence against your brother Jacob, Shame shall cover you, And you shall be cut off forever. [11]In the day that you stood on the other side— In the day that strangers carried captive his forces when foreigners entered his gates And cast lots for Jerusalem— Even you were as one of them. [12]"But you should not have gazed on

> the day of your brother In the day of his captivity; Nor should you have rejoiced over the children of Judah In the day of their destruction; Nor should you have spoken proudly In the day of distress. [13]You should not have entered the gate of My people In the day of their calamity. Indeed, you should not have gazed on their affliction In the day of their calamity, Nor laid hands on their substance In the day of their calamity. [14]You should not have stood at the crossroads To cut off those among them who escaped; Nor should you have delivered up those among them who remained In the day of distress. [15]"For the day of the LORD upon all the nations is near; As you have done, it shall be done to you; Your reprisal shall return upon your own head. [16]For as you drank on My holy mountain, So shall all the nations drink continually; Yes, they shall drink and swallow, And they shall be as though they had never been. —Obadiah 1:10-16

God's reason stems clear back to Esau's mistreatment of Jacob and then fast forwards to the time of the Babylonian captivity and the treatment of Israel by Esau's descendants. They participated in the looting of Jerusalem and God's people and rejoiced over their brothers' demise. They also helped the invaders by capturing and turning over any that were fleeing from the attack. This betrayal was very odious to God. In verse 15 and following, the prophet fast forwarded again to a period near the end of the age, even leading up to the day of the Lord. At the second coming of the Lord, the armies of the nations will be gathered on the same mountains to drink of the judgment of God, and they will be remembered no more.

In verses 17-20, there is a stark contrast between what will happen to the nations of the confederacy and what will happen to Israel. Instead of divine judgment, Israel will receive divine deliverance from her enemies. Let me be very clear. This deliverance would be absolutely impossible without God supernaturally intervening in the natural life of Israel and her enemies. The prophet says that Israel will finally possess their possessions. He says that the house of Israel will be a fire and a flame and the house of Esau shall be stubble. He goes on to say that the house of Esau will be devoured and that no survivor shall remain. At that time, Israel shall possess the fields of all those who, as part of the confederacy, conspired against them.

> 17"But on Mount Zion, there shall be deliverance, And
> there shall be holiness; The house of Jacob shall pos-
> sess their possessions. 18The house of Jacob shall be a
> fire, And the house of Joseph a flame; But the house
> of Esau shall be stubble; They shall kindle them and
> devour them, And no survivor shall remain of the
> house of Esau," For the LORD has spoken. 19The South
> shall possess the mountains of Esau, And the Lowland
> shall possess Philistia. They shall possess the fields of
> Ephraim And the fields of Samaria. Benjamin shall pos-
> sess Gilead. 20And the captives of this host of the chil-
> dren of Israel Shall possess the land of the Canaanites
> As far as Zarephath. The captives of Jerusalem who are
> in Sepharad shall possess the cities of the South.
>
> —Obadiah 1:17-20

More On "Why Judgment Comes?"

As we reflect more on why judgment comes upon people, families, and even nations, it is essential to realize how important the choices we make really are. Our decisions not only affect our lives but also the lives of those around us, especially those with whom we bear a relationship, whether by blood or choice. Our choices often affect not only the relationships in our generation but also those of future generations. Look at what God says in Deuteronomy 30:19.

> [19]I call heaven and earth as witnesses today against you, that I have set before you life and death, blessing and cursing; therefore choose life, that both you and your descendants may live. —Deuteronomy 30:19

Life and death, blessing and cursing are choices we must make. God wants us to choose life and blessing. The Scriptures also make clear that our decisions can result in blessing and cursing continuing onto our descendants for three or four generations after we have died. It is sobering to think that my choices can affect not only my children but even my great, great grandchildren! I certainly want to pass down blessing rather than cursing. If none of the four generations that follow me make choices that reverse what I have passed down, then the potential of my choices, whether blessing or cursing, may continue in perpetuity (the state of endlessness). Wow! That's a sobering thought.

With that in mind, let's take a closer look as to why the judgments will be leveled on the people of the confederacy of Psalm 83. There are many Scriptures that we could look at, but for our study let's look at a passage in Ezekiel 25. The first part of this chapter dealt with a period of judgment in the Middle East nations when Nebuchadnezzar was waging war to expand his kingdom. The second part deals with judgment in a period near the end of the age, albeit by the hand of a different aggressor. This passage makes clear that though the rods in God's hand bringing the judgments were different, the choices that brought both judgments were not.

> 1The word of the LORD came to me, saying, 2"Son of man, set your face against the Ammonites, and prophesy against them. 3Say to the Ammonites, 'Hear the word of the Lord GOD! Thus says the Lord GOD: "Because you said, 'Aha!' against My sanctuary when it was profaned, and against the land of Israel when it was desolate, and against the house of Judah when they went into captivity, 4indeed, therefore, I will deliver you as a possession to the men of the East, and they shall set their encampments among you and make their dwellings among you; they shall eat your fruit, and they shall drink your milk. 5And I will make Rabbah a stable for camels and Ammon a resting place for flocks. Then you shall know that I am the LORD." 6'For thus says the Lord GOD: "Because you clapped your hands, stamped your feet, and rejoiced in heart with all your disdain for the land of Israel, 7indeed, therefore, I will stretch out My hand against you, and give you as plunder to the nations; I will cut you off from the peoples, and I will cause you to perish from the countries; I will destroy you, and you shall know that I am the LORD." 8'Thus says the Lord

> GOD: "Because Moab and Seir say, 'Look! The house of Judah is like all the nations,' [9]therefore, behold, I will clear the territory of Moab of cities, of the cities on its frontier, the glory of the country, Beth Jeshimoth, Baal Meon, and Kirjathaim. [10]To the men of the East I will give it as a possession, together with the Ammonites, that the Ammonites may not be remembered among the nations. [11]And I will execute judgments upon Moab, and they shall know that I am the LORD."
>
> —Ezekiel 25:1-11

This passage shows that God was not pleased with the choices made by these various people groups and nations. The result of these choices was cursing, ultimately leading to the judgment of God on their lives. He told the Ammonites that because they said, "Aha" and then clapped their hands, stamped their feet, and rejoiced in their heart with disdain over the land of Israel, He would stretch out His hand of judgment and give them as plunder to the nations. The very same aggressor they once looked so favorably on was used by God to judge them, too. Moab and Seir resented the apparent fact that Israel was a unique, chosen people blessed by God. When Israel fell, they took great satisfaction in declaring that Israel was not so special after all but rather like all the other nations. This attitude brought the same judgment by the same aggressor on them, too.

Though the second part of this passage continues with the theme of judgment because of bad choices, it reflects a sudden change in context concerning the time period in which the judgments would occur and who God would use to mete out those judgments. As you read this next passage, I encourage you to identify these contextual differences before you continue reading this book.

> 12'Thus says the Lord GOD: "Because of what Edom did against the house of Judah by taking vengeance, and has greatly offended by avenging itself on them," 13therefore thus says the Lord GOD: "I will also stretch out My hand against Edom, cut off man and beast from it, and make it desolate from Teman; Dedan shall fall by the sword. 14I will lay My vengeance on Edom by the hand of My people Israel, that they may do in Edom according to My anger and according to My fury; and they shall know My vengeance," says the Lord GOD. 15'Thus says the Lord GOD: "Because the Philistines dealt vengefully and took vengeance with a spiteful heart, to destroy because of the old hatred," 16therefore thus says the Lord GOD: "I will stretch out My hand against the Philistines, and I will cut off the Cherethites and destroy the remnant of the seacoast. 17I will execute great vengeance on them with furious rebukes, and they shall know that I am the LORD when I lay My vengeance upon them."' "
>
> —Ezekiel 25:12-17

Notice that the judgment against Edom (Esau) was for past choices, but the judgment leveled was being reaped in another generation near the end of the age. In verse 14, God makes clear that the judgments He would inflict will be by the hand of His people, Israel, and not Nebuchadnezzar. This is clearly speaking of a different time than that of the Babylonian captivity, which was to serve as a typological fulfillment of an ultimate fulfillment reserved for the end of the age. I believe this is about the Psalm 83 war that will unfold very shortly. He said He would utterly destroy man and beast from Teman, which is in Jordan, all the way to Dedan, which is in Saudi Arabia. The prophet then begins to speak to the Philistines, who have until this present day dwelt in the Gaza Strip. He informs them that the impending judgments are the result of previous choices and attitudes by a generation who long ago took vengeance on Israel with cruelty. He even cites past hatreds as the reason for this generation's determination to vengefully set out to destroy Israel. He said it was because of past animosities. Because they did not make choices that would reverse the curses of the past, they passed these curses on to future generations. This prophecy indicates that none of the subsequent generations made decisions to move them from cursing to blessing. Even to this day, there is still hateful animosity by these people toward Israel. These are the very people who have been launching rockets into Israeli cities and committing acts of terrorism for the past several decades. God will use the coming judgments to cause these nations of the confederacy to know that He is the true God, not Allah.

Nature of the Judgment

As we conclude our study of the Psalm 83 war, bear with me as I engage in some speculation as to how these judgments might unfold. I will make every attempt to base my speculative scenarios on my interpretations of related biblical passages. So let's begin.

The first scenario involves the judgments on Syria and its capital city, Damascus. Isaiah 25 prophesied about this in verses 2-5. Before we begin to look at this passage, I want to share a few thoughts about verse 1. In this verse, the prophet opened by praising God for the extraordinary things He has done, even though their fulfillments are yet to come. This is to make evident that His counsels of old are based on His faithfulness as well as truth. It proves that He watches over His words to perform them as spoken. Once God speaks, it is as good as done. He will not alter it once it has passed His lips. He calls those things which are not as though they already are. It is interesting that the Hebrew language does not have a future tense but instead utilizes a prophetic perfect tense. For example, the prophecy stating a virgin shall conceive, bear a son, and call His name Emanuel would read differently in Hebrew. In the prophetic perfect tense, it would read, "A virgin has conceived, born a son, and has called His name Emanuel." I say all of this to make the point that the blessings and cursings of the past are still in play today unless they are reversed by a return to or a departure from the faith.

I have included the Isaiah passage below so that you can read it before I begin to share my speculative thoughts.

> 2For You have made a city a ruin, A fortified city a ruin, A palace of foreigners to be a city no more; It will never be rebuilt. 3Therefore the strong people will glorify You; The city of the terrible nations will fear You. 4For You have been a strength to the poor, a strength to the needy in his distress, A refuge from the storm, A shade from

> the heat; For the blast of the terrible ones is as a storm against the wall. [5]You will reduce the noise of aliens, As heat in a dry place; As heat in the shadow of a cloud, The song of the terrible ones will be diminished.
>
> —Isaiah 25:2-5

First of all, let me say that I believe this passage is speaking of the Psalm 83 war. Though the name of the city is not disclosed here, I will show from other passages that this is talking about the city of Damascus, Syria. It says that God will make this fortified city and palace (capital) a ruin that will never be rebuilt. In that day, the strong people (Israel) will glorify God while the people of the terrible nations (confederacy) will fear God. Verse 4 speaks of how God has been a strength to the poor and needy and a refuge from the storm. I feel this is speaking of Israel being under an attack initiated by Syria. I personally believe this attack will involve weapons of mass destruction. The next phrase says that God will be a shade from the heat because the blast of the terrible ones comes like a storm against a wall. Could this be describing the heat from a nuclear explosion or some other weapon of mass destruction that God supernaturally puts up a barrier to absorb? I remind you that He foiled the attack of Pharaoh at the Red Sea with a wall of fire. We know that Syria has weapons of mass destruction that they have already used. Since Russia and Iran are now militarily entrenched in Syria, they would have access to nuclear weapons. Whatever the attack involved, verse 5 describes Israel's response to this aggression as one that would reduce the noise of the foreigners. Remember in Psalm 83 that the people of the confederacy made a tumultuous noise and lifted up their heads against God and His people, Israel. Verse 5 goes on to give us clues as to the nature of Israel's military response. It says that they reduced the noise of their enemies as heat in a dry place; as heat in the shadow of a cloud resulting in the song of the terrible ones being diminished. To me, this sounds like a nuclear attack (heat) in a dry place such as Syria and as heat in the shadow of a nuclear cloud. Would Israel resort to the nuclear option? Keep in mind the world is increasingly becoming more and more antagonistic and aggressive toward Israel. Even the US's commitment to them is waning. If Syria used weapons of mass destruction, Israel would have nothing to lose by pulling out all the stops. We know prophetically speaking that one day the whole world will align themselves against Israel. I see no other choice for them. Their nuclear capabilities would be the only option when being placed in such a predicament. Allow me to continue to speculate as we look at another related Scripture passage found in Isaiah.

> 1The burden against Damascus. "Behold, Damascus will
> cease from being a city, And it will be a ruinous heap.
> 2The cities of Aroer are forsaken; They will be for flocks
> Which lie down, and no one will make them afraid.
>
> —Isaiah 17:1-2

Here the name of the city that will be a ruinous heap and cease to exist is identified as Damascus. Though what is described here cannot be positively identified as a nuclear blast, it certainly cannot be ruled out, either. Remember, atomic warfare would not be a part of Isaiah's experience or vocabulary. He would have to describe it and its effects from what he could relate to and see. It goes on to say that the cities in the region around Damascus were deserted because the people were afraid that the demise of Damascus might soon be their plight, too. These cities were so void of humans that the animals had full run of the cities because there was no one left to spook them or make them afraid. As we read on in this passage, we will see that Israel, though protected by God from total destruction, did not go altogether unscathed.

> 3The fortress also will cease from Ephraim, The kingdom
> from Damascus, And the remnant of Syria; They will be
> as the glory of the children of Israel," Says the LORD of
> hosts. 4"In that day it shall come to pass That the glory of
> Jacob will wane, And the fatness of his flesh grow lean.
> 5It shall be as when the harvester gathers the grain and
> reaps the heads with his arm; It shall be as he who gath-
> ers heads of grain In the Valley of Rephaim. 6Yet gleaning
> grapes will be left in it, Like the shaking of an olive tree,
> Two or three olives at the top of the uppermost bough,
> Four or five in its most fruitful branches," Says the LORD
> God of Israel. 7In that day a man will look to his Maker,
> And his eyes will have respect for the Holy One of Israel.
> 8He will not look to the altars, The work of his hands;
> He will not respect what his fingers have made, Nor the
> wooden images nor the incense altars. 9In that day his
> strong cities will be as a forsaken bough And an upper-
> most branch, Which they left because of the children of
> Israel; And there will be desolation. 10Because you have
> forgotten the God of your salvation, And have not been

> mindful of the Rock of your stronghold, Therefore you will plant pleasant plants and set out foreign seedlings;
> 11In the day you will make your plant to grow, And in the morning you will make your seed to flourish; But the harvest will be a heap of ruins In the day of grief and desperate sorrow. —Isaiah 17:3-11

This passage begins by saying the fortress of Ephraim will cease, as will the kingdom from Damascus and the remnant of Syria. Ephraim has often been used as a reference to the northern part of the nation of Israel. It was known by the dominant tribe inhabiting that area, Ephraim. To me, a fortress is symbolic of how people can find the protection to dwell safely while giving them a vantage point from which they can war effectively. I believe this passage speaks of the destruction resulting from military engagements involving weapons of mass destruction on both sides. It describes Syria as having the same level of reduced glory as Israel was experiencing at that time. Verse 4 begins to explain how the glory or condition of northern Israel had greatly diminished as a result of the devastation inflicted by Syria. God's judgments affected both Syria and Ephraim alike. I believe Ephraim's punishment was a result of choices made many years before when they sided with the Syrians to fight against Judah. Remember, decisions have consequences no matter how long ago they were made, unless they are undone with godly choices later.

Let's look closely at how the prophet describes the devastation of northern Israel in the aftermath of God's judgment. It says that the fatness of their flesh will grow lean, which suggests not only the lack of food but also of the ability to produce it. He says the harvest will be like the aftermath of reaping in the valley of Rephaim, which is the valley of the giants. There was not much left after the giants harvested. There were just a few gleanings of grapes and olives. It says explicitly that there were only two or three olives left on the top of the uppermost branches and only four or five in the most fruitful branches. Food will be scarce, and there will be desolation. They were under the curse of God because they forgot that He was the rock of their salvation and their stronghold. He says that even though they would import quality seeds and seedlings, their harvest would be a heap of ruins causing them much grief and desperate sorrow. This seems to indicate that the attack by Syria was such that it not only affected the people but also the land where they dwelt. These conditions convince me even more strongly that a nuclear attack was the reason for such total devastation. Conventional warfare may destroy cities, but it would not render the soil incapable of growing a good harvest, especially if good seed and seedlings were imported and planted.

As was the glory and fate of northern Israel, so was the fate of Damascus, Syria, and her surviving remnant. Verses 7-9 echoes this truth in saying Syria will no longer look to their idols but instead will have respect for the Holy One of Israel. In that day, their strong cities will be abandoned as they leave them because of the children of Israel. This shows that Israel is the cause of their desolation.

The prophet then proceeded in verses 12-14 to speak to the other nations of the confederacy, who I am persuaded will react to Israel's devastating attack on Syria.

> [12]Woe to the multitude of many people Who make a noise like the roar of the seas, And to the rushing of nations That make a rushing like the rushing of mighty waters! [13]The nations will rush like the rushing of many waters; But God will rebuke them, and they will flee far away, and be chased like the chaff of the mountains before the wind, like a rolling thing before the whirlwind. [14]Then behold, at eventide, trouble! And before the morning, he is no more. This is the portion of those who plunder us and the lot of those who rob us.
>
> —Isaiah 17:12-14

I believe Syria's demise will not change the confederacy's plan to cut Israel off from being a nation as depicted in Psalm 83. Though there will be many that assemble themselves against Israel at night, they will not prevail against her. God will rebuke them that night so that by morning they will all flee as Israel chases them. Israel serves the world notice that this will be the portion of any other nation who tries to plunder and rob them. Isaiah, chapters 26-28, gives more details concerning the judgments of the other countries of the Psalm 83 coalition.

In conclusion, a thought to consider is, "What do you think the response of the UN and its member nations will be to the results of the Psalm 83 war?"

CHAPTER 16

Gog and Magog

Introduction

Though I contend that the wars of Psalm 83 and Gog and Magog are not the same, they are very closely related. As a matter of fact, I am convinced the Psalm 83 war will precipitate the war of Gog and Magog as a swift response to Israel's astonishing military victory. I believe it will be the reason the onlooking world will do no more than question the Russian/Iranian-led coalition as to their motives, rather than militarily resist their invasion of Israel. It would be no surprise if the United Nations and the news media around the world will be unified in condemning Israel's actions as unmitigated, baseless aggression. This will cause the opinion polls of the nations to reach unprecedented lows concerning Israel's favorability. The reality will be that the real aggressors are Russia and Iran, who instigate and fight this proxy war through the nations that immediately surround Israel. The battle of Gog and Magog will expose this coalition's true motives. However, the alliance they form will be so formidable that the nations will be afraid to challenge it militarily.

The "Who" of the War

Now let's identify the nations that make up this coalition as described in Ezekiel chapter 38.

> [1]Now the word of the LORD came to me, saying, [2]"Son
> of man, set your face against Gog, of the land of Magog, the prince of Rosh, Meshech, and Tubal, and prophesy
> against him, [3]and say, 'Thus says the Lord GOD: "Behold, I am against you, O Gog, the prince of Rosh, Meshech,
> and Tubal. [4]I will turn you around, put hooks into your jaws, and lead you out, with all your army, horses, and horsemen, all splendidly clothed, a great company with bucklers and shields, all of them handling swords.
> [5]Persia, Ethiopia, and Libya are with them, all of them
> with shield and helmet; [6]Gomer and all its troops; the
> house of Togarmah from the far north and all its troops-many people are with you. —Ezekiel 38:1-6

There has been much debate about what modern-day countries will be a part of the confederacy who will come against Israel in the battle of Gog and Magog. I don't want to join this debate because I feel its significance is much overrated as to how the prophecy plays out. I am more interested in the major players who will be involved and not those countries who will accompany them. Though there is some debate even over who the major players are, I will take the liberty of sharing my view on this without spending vast amounts of time and space in this book supporting the basis of my conclusions. There is much research material available whereby you can draw your own conclusions. Regardless of who will and who will not participate in this alliance, it does not change the fact that a confederacy will come against Israel in the last days. The outcome will be as prophesied irrespective of what nations are involved. And now let's begin to identify these countries and people groups that I believe will make up this confederacy.

In doing so, what hermeneutic should one use in making this determination? Should we look at the people and places in which they dwelt at the time of the writing of this prophecy or should we look at the people and their dwelling places at the time of the end of the age? The Scriptures in Ezekiel 38 describe people groups and also geographical regions or nations.

First, let me speak as to the timing. I believe the prophet was seeing an event that would occur near the end of the age using as descriptors things he understood concerning peoples and places during his lifetime. To take an identified people group of his day and assume they have not migrated but remained in the same geographical location until the time of the unfolding of the prophecy would be a mistake. It is important to remember that after the flood, the world was populated through the three sons of Noah migrating into all the world. However, when speaking of countries, I think we should interpret them literally even though their borders might have changed many times from the time of Ezekiel unto the end of the age. For example, though her boundaries may have changed somewhat, Egypt still refers to Egypt.

From the above passage we see that the leader of Russia (Magog) along with other former USSR nations (Rosh, Meshech, and Tubal) will join with the likes of Iran (Persia), Eritrea and Sudan (Ethiopia), Libya, Tunisia, Morocco and Algeria (Libya), Germany and Allies (Gomer), and Turkey (Togarmah).

This raises the question, "Does God just arbitrarily choose the nations of this confederacy or is His choice based on cause and effect?" The answer can be found in the Scriptures. Jeremiah declares that God is going to make a full end of the nations to which Israel was scattered – Jeremiah 30:11,16,24.

> [11]For I am with you,' says the LORD, 'to save you; Though I make a full end of all nations where I have scattered you, Yet I will not make a complete end of you. But I will correct you in justice, And will not let you go altogether unpunished.' [16]'Therefore all those who devour you shall be devoured; And all your adversaries, every one of them, shall go into captivity; Those who plunder you shall become plunder, and all who prey upon you I will make a prey. [24]The fierce anger of the LORD will not return until He has done it, and until He has performed the intents of His heart. In the latter days, you will consider it.
>
> —Jeremiah 30:11,16,24

Notice that those who devour Israel will be devoured; those who plunder Israel shall be plundered. This supports the notion of "cause and effect" that I mentioned earlier as being God's basis of gathering these particular nations against Israel. What two countries have slaughtered more

Jews than Germany and Russia? What nation is any more determined to annihilate Israel today than Iran (Persia)? Many of those nations have been a continual thorn in the side of Israel for years. It is God who will put a hook in the jaw of those nations to come against Israel, that they might go into the long-awaited judgment of God.

The "Where" of the War

The "Where" of the war is clearly defined in Ezekiel 38:8 as being the land of Israel after she has been regathered from the nations. I also believe that her borders will then be expanded to the post-Psalm 83 war boundaries as prophetically promised to Abraham.

> 8After many days you will be visited. In the latter years, you will come into the land of those brought back from the sword and gathered from many people on the mountains of Israel, which had long been desolate; they were brought out of the nations, and now all of them dwell safely. —Ezekiel 38:8

This Scripture leaves no doubt that armies of the confederacy stage their offensive to attack Israel on the very mountains of Israel.

The "When" of the War

The "When" of the war can be seen in Ezekiel 38:8,11,14.

> 8After many days you will be visited. In the latter years, you will come into the land of those brought back from

> the sword and gathered from many people on the mountains of Israel, which had long been desolate; they were brought out of the nations, and now all of them dwell safely. [11]You will say, 'I will go up against a land of unwalled villages; I will go to a peaceful people, who dwell safely, all of them dwelling without walls, and having neither bars nor gates. [14]"Therefore, son of man, prophesy and say to Gog, 'Thus says the Lord GOD: "On that day when My people Israel dwell safely, will you not know it?
>
> —Ezekiel 38:8,11,14

Notice that the above passage is referencing the period after Israel has been regathered as a nation after having been scattered throughout the earth in 70 AD. God clearly states that this event will happen in the latter days. It is a time in Israel's history when she will occupy her land in peace and safety. This has not happened since she was repatriated in 1948 until this present time. However, the Bible prophesies that this will happen in the last days. I believe that time-span will begin after the conclusion of the Psalm 83 war and will continue until the beginning of the battle of Gog and Magog and possibly beyond. Ezekiel confirms this in the 28th chapter:

> [24]"And there shall no longer be a pricking brier or a painful thorn for the house of Israel from among all who are around them, whodespise them. Then they shall know that I am the Lord GOD." [25]'Thus says the Lord GOD: "When I have gathered the house of Israel from the peoples among whom they are scattered, and am hallowed in them in the sight of the Gentiles, then they

> will dwell in their own land which I gave to My servant Jacob. [26]And they will dwell safely there, build houses, and plant vineyards; yes, they will dwell securely, when I execute judgments on all those around them who despise them. Then they shall know that I am the LORD their God."
> —Ezekiel 28:24-26

I believe Jeremiah 30:24 also speaks of this very event.

> [24]The fierce anger of the LORD will not return until He has done it, and until He has performed the intents of His heart. In the latter days, you will consider it.
> —Jeremiah 30:24

The "Why" of the War

I believe the Scriptures are clear as to the motive of Russia in coming against Israel in the latter days.

> [12]to take plunder and to take booty, to stretch out your hand against the waste places that are again inhabited, and against a people gathered from the nations, who have acquired livestock and goods, who dwell in the midst of the land. [13]Sheba, Dedan, the merchants of Tarshish, and all their young lions will say to you, 'Have you come to take plunder? Have you gathered your army to take booty, to carry away silver and gold, to take away livestock and goods, to take great plunder?'
> —Ezekiel 38:12-13

Verse 12 exposes that the primary motive of Russia is like that of taking plunder and booty. Though Iran and several other nations of the confederacy might be more motivated by ideology propagated by radical Islamic theology, Russia is motivated by greed and power. They will be seeking to be engorged by what Israel has to offer. What does Israel have that Russia will be lusting after? What would be the hook in the jaw that draws her into Israel?

Though the text of the above passage identifies some of the spoil the confederacy is interested in (silver, gold, livestock and goods), the great plunder is not clearly defined. To understand the nature of the hook that pulls them into Israel, we have to consider Israel's discoveries in the latter days. A prophetic hint of these discoveries can be seen in various Old Testament Scriptures. I am listing several of them below for your consideration.

> [11]I will multiply upon you man and beast, and they shall increase and bear young; I will make you inhabited as in former times, and do better for you than at your beginnings. Then you shall know that I am the LORD.
>
> —Ezekiel 36:11

> [13]And of Joseph, he said: "Blessed of the LORD is his land,
> with the precious things of heaven, with the dew, and
> the deep lying beneath [14]With the precious fruits of the
> sun, With the precious produce of the months, [15]With
> the best things of the ancient mountains, with the pre-
> cious things of the everlasting hills, [16]With the precious
> things of the earth. [19]They shall call the peoples to the
> mountain; There they shall offer sacrifices of righteous-
> ness; For they shall partake of the abundance of the seas
> and of treasures hidden in the sand." [24]And of Asher, he

> said: "Asher is most blessed of sons; Let him be favored by his brothers, And let him dip his foot in oil.
> —Deuteronomy 33:13-16,19,24

> [3]I will give you the treasures of darkness And hidden riches of secret places, That you may know that I, the LORD, Who call you by your name, Am the God of Israel. —Isaiah 45:3

> [25]By the God of your father who will help you, And by the Almighty who will bless you with blessings of heaven above, Blessings of the deep that lies beneath, Blessings of the breasts and of the womb.
> —Genesis 49:25

I believe the recent developments in Israel are that which were spoken or prophesied by the Scriptures above. What are some of the latest discoveries of which I speak?

In 2009, the Tamar gas field was discovered in the Mediterranean Sea off Israel's coast. The very next year, the Leviathan gas and oil fields were found some thirty miles southwest of the Tamar field. The estimates of these two discoveries are continually being adjusted upwards. It is now estimated that these fields contain four billion barrels of oil and over thirteen trillion cubic feet of natural gas. If that weren't enough, the discovery of oil in the Golan Heights is so extensive that it is estimated that Israel will be a major world player in the oil and natural gas market. Together, the wealth of these recent discoveries have already piqued international interest. Why?

Let's consider Russia, the primary payer in this confederacy. Russia's most significant economic resource of natural gas has also been used as a weapon to influence and manipulate much of Europe. Europe gets almost half of its natural gas from Russia. Because of her vulnerability, Europe began looking at two alternative gas pipelines that would bypass Russia. One route began at Qatar and passed through Syria to the Mediterranean Sea. The other route started in Iran and passed through Syria to the sea, also. The pipeline from Russia to European nations runs through Ukraine. In 2009 during the Ukrainian Civil War, Russia did what Europe feared. She shut off the pipeline to Europe to counter the US and European sanctions imposed because of Russia's deliberate military aggression in Ukraine. Europe shivered in the dark and was left entirely at the mercy of Russia. Now they know that Russia will not hesitate to blackmail them whenever their actions displease the Kremlin's interests on the world stage. However, with these new discoveries, Russia's greatest fear is that Israel, now having become a major world exporter of energy, will build a pipeline into Europe. This would be a faster and less expensive option for Europe than the previously two considered routes through Syria. This would result in Russia losing its advantage of being able to control the behavior of her neighbors to the West in reaction to her geopolitical aspirations. If Russia can manufacture a reason to attack and defeat Israel, she would use the spoils of war to control a large sector of the energy market and become a dominant world superpower. This is what she wants. This is why she is currently in Syria. She wants a land bridge from her southern border through Iran all the way to the Mediterranean Sea. She hopes to use Israel's antagonistic surrounding neighbors to fight a proxy war for her to gain this advantage. However, when this endeavor fails as described in the Psalm 83 war, she will herself form an overwhelming formidable alliance of nations to achieve her goal. As with the proxy war, so too will this act of aggression fail to gain her the greedy, diabolical intents of her heart. We need to keep our eyes on the Middle East and especially on Syria.

Is it just a coincidence that both Russia and Iran are now strategically entrenched in Syria? Their motives are not humanitarian, for sure. God is using their evil intentions to fulfill that which He spoke prophetically over two thousand years ago. Soon He will be setting the hook in the jaw of the Gog and Magog confederacy. May we not forget that two nations of this alliance, Russia and Germany, are responsible for the murder of over seven million (???) Jews in the last century. You can be sure God has not forgotten. God watches over His Word to perform it, that not one word of it will fail to come to pass, even as He prophesied it would.

If all of these riches weren't enough, you also have a wealth of untapped treasures in the Dead Sea. Its waters contain billions of tons of sodium, magnesium, potassium, chlorine, bromide, and calcium. These minerals are precious in the world market. Can you imagine in your mind a picture of Russia and her allies looking wistfully at the land of Israel with their tongues hanging out with greed?

The "What" of the War

Under the topic of the "What" of the war, I will discuss what actually happens during this war and what the final outcome will be.

In the first nine verses of Ezekiel 38, God identifies a confederacy led primarily by the prince/leader of Russia & former Soviet states. In verses six and fifteen, God says that Gog will bring his armies from the far north. Again in verse two of Ezekiel 39, He reiterates that Gog will come from the far north. It is interesting to note that Moscow is approximately 1,700 miles north of Jerusalem.

> [6]Gomer and all its troops; the house of Togarmah from the far north and all its troops-many people are with you. [15]Then you will come from your place out of the far north, you and many peoples with you, all of them riding on horses, a great company and a mighty army.
>
> —Ezekiel 38:6,15

> [1]"And you, son of man, prophesy against Gog, and say, 'Thus says the Lord GOD: "Behold, I am against you, O Gog, the prince of Rosh, Meshech, and Tubal; [2]and I will turn you around and lead you on, bringing you up from the far north, and bring you against the mountains of Israel. —Ezekiel 39:1-2

In these passages, the Lord makes clear He is against this prince. In the previous pages, I discussed the motives of the various nations to wage war against Israel. Let me suggest to you what God's motivation will be for this war. I believe the remembrance by God of the atrocities perpetrated against Israel by previous generations is the underlying motive for His drawing Russia into this battle. God says that He will put a hook in the jaw of the leaders of Russia and other nations for the express purpose of bringing them into a place of judgment. He prophesies that Russia will ascend, coming like a storm, covering the land like a cloud with all of her troops along with many soldiers from the other nations in alliance with her.

In Ezekiel 38:10-11, God says that in that day, thoughts would arise in Gog's mind and he would devise an evil plan. This plan would be to attack a land of unwalled villages against a peaceful people dwelling safely without walls or fences. This not only identifies the nation of Israel but depicts a time when Israel will no longer be harassed with terrorism and aggression by surrounding countries. This will result in Israel no longer needing security fences and walls to daily protect herself from her hateful neighbors. Obviously, this is not Israel's current reality. However, after the Psalm 83 war, which I believe will begin to unfold in the not too distant future, this will become her current reality.

In verses 12-13, the motive of Gog is revealed as that of the desire to take plunder or spoils of war from Israel, as I have mentioned earlier in this chapter. Even other nations, such as Sheba, Dedan, the merchants of Tarshish, and all their young lions, will question her motive and ask if she is coming to take "great plunder." "Great Plunder" reinforces the fact that Israel will have discovered great treasures that are the envy of the world. Most scholars agree that Sheba and Dedan make up what we now call Saudi Arabia. Though there are divided opinions as to who Tarshish is, I personally believe Tarshish represents the UK and all her young lions that once were a part of her United Kingdom, such as the US, Canada, Australia, and New Zealand. Again, more important than the exact identities of the players is what will happen in the world as a result of this prophecy of Ezekiel.

In verses 14-16, God begins to prophesy specifically over Gog as to when and how this war will unfold. Let there be no doubt, it will come to pass even as the prophecy states. God watches over His Word to perform it.

> [14]"Therefore, son of man, prophesy and say to Gog, 'Thus says the Lord GOD: "On that day when My people Israel dwell safely, will you not know it? [15]Then you will come from your place out of the far north, you and many peoples with you, all of them riding on horses, a great company and a mighty army. [16]You will come up against My people Israel like a cloud, to cover the land. It will be in the latter days that I will bring you against My land, so that the nations may know Me, when I am hallowed in you, O Gog, before their eyes." —Ezekiel 38:14-16

Notice that God reiterates the timing of this war by saying it will be on the very day in which His people, Israel, dwell safely. When Gog realizes that his plan to gain access to Israel's wealth through the proxy Psalm 83 war fails, he must come up with a plan B. This is when Gog will devise a plan to come against Israel directly in what is referred to as "the battle of Gog and Magog."

Gog will come with a mighty army so vast that it will be like a cloud covering the land of Israel. God declares that He will bring this army to His land so the nations will take notice of the glory of God through the mighty acts they see Him do.

God goes on to say that when Gog comes against Israel, His fury will become evident. In jealousy, God will unleash the fire of His wrath with a great earthquake. It will be so violent that everything in the sea, sky, and earth will shake at the presence of God. The mountains will fall, causing enormous landslides, and the walls of the buildings will collapse.

> [18]"And it will come to pass at the same time when Gog comes against the land of Israel," says the Lord GOD, "that My fury will show in My face. [19]For in My jealousy and in the fire of My wrath I have spoken: 'Surely in that day there shall be a great earthquake in the land of Israel, [20]so that the fish of the sea, the birds of the heavens, the beasts of the field, all creeping things that creep on the earth, and all men who are on the face of the earth shall shake at My presence. The mountains shall be thrown down, the steep places shall fall, and every wall shall fall to the ground.' —Ezekiel 38:18-20

As the earth shakes at the presence of God, He will call for a sword against Gog and his armies. The earthquake will create such fear and confusion that soldiers of the confederacy will turn against each other. God will also send pestilence, bloodshed, flooding rain, great hailstones, fire, and brimstone. In so doing, God will devastate the armies of

Gog and magnify Himself in the eyes of many nations. They will truly know that He is Lord!

> [22]And I will bring him to judgment with pestilence and bloodshed; I will rain down on him, on his troops, and on the many peoples who are with him, flooding rain, great hailstones, fire, and brimstone. [23]Thus I will magnify Myself and sanctify Myself, and I will be known in the eyes of many nations. Then they shall know that I am the LORD."' —Ezekiel 38:22-23

Though God and the nations of the confederacy each had their own goals for this war, the end result will be that only God's intentions are realized. Though on the world scene the battle being staged looks like a slam dunk for the confederacy and sure destruction for Israel, God miraculously comes to the rescue of Israel, while at the same time judging the very nations who have mistreated God's people for centuries.

In Ezekiel 39, God instructs the prophet to prophesy again to reinforce to all that whatever God speaks shall surely come to pass. He foretells the devastating destruction on Gog and all that are with him. I include the first five verses of chapter 39 in the KJV version to illustrate a point not seen in other translations. In verse 2, the Greek word *shawshaw* means "to annihilate or to leave the sixth part of." This can be seen in Strong's Concordance. Why other translations don't include this fact is puzzling to me.

> [1]Therefore, thou son of man, prophesy against Gog, and say, Thus saith the Lord GOD; Behold, I am against thee,

> O Gog, the chief prince of Meshech and Tubal: [2]And I will turn thee back and leave but the sixth part of thee, and will cause thee to come up from the north parts and will bring thee upon the mountains of Israel: [3]And I will smite thy bow out of thy left hand, and will cause thine arrows to fall out of thy right hand. [4]Thou shalt fall upon the mountains of Israel, thou, and all thy bands, and the people that is with thee: I will give thee unto the ravenous birds of every sort, and to the beasts of the field to be devoured [5]Thou shalt fall upon the open field: for I have spoken it, saith the Lord GOD.
>
> —Ezekiel 39:1-5 (KJV)

God says their bodies will become food for the birds and the beasts to devour.

The prophecy goes on to declare that not only the armies will come under the judgment of God, but so also will His fiery judgments be experienced by the people in the nations represented by these armies. In other words, judgment will not be limited to the geographical area of Israel but also will fall in Russia, Iran, and in all the countries participating in the confederacy. Then the nations will know that He is God and the Holy One of Israel.

> [6]"And I will send fire on Magog and on those who live in security in the coastlands. Then they shall know that I am the LORD. [7]So I will make My holy name known in the midst of My people Israel, and I will not let them profane My holy name anymore. Then the nations shall know that I am the LORD, the Holy One in Israel. [8]Surely it is coming, and it shall be done," says the Lord GOD.

"This is the day of which I have spoken.

—Ezekiel 39:6-8

The rest of chapter 39 of Ezekiel deals with the aftermath of the battle, which concludes before they can execute their plan. For brevity's sake, I will make comments on the highlights of this passage.

In a single day, God destroys 5/6th of Gog's massive army without Israel having to fire a shot. The devastation is so great that Israel will be seven months burying the dead bodies and seven years burning the leftovers of war. Israel will not have to use any of their own fuel and other provisions because the spoils of war will provide many of her needs. She will end up robbing those who intended to rob her of resources. She will plunder those who come to take plunder. That will be kind of ironic. The fact that they will be consuming the spoils of their attackers for seven years means that this battle must take place before the last seven years of this age begin. I personally believe that the conclusion of this war will precipitate the beginning of the Great Tribulation. The mighty acts of God to save His people, Israel, against insurmountable odds of inevitable defeat will cause Israel to know that the Lord is her God from that day forward. God will make known to Israel and to the heathens that the house of Israel went into captivity because of their iniquity. It is because they trespassed against the Lord that He hid His face from them and gave them into the hand of their enemies in times past. It will be clear His punishment of them is over, and it was God and not the United Nations that brought them back from captivity to once again inhabit their own land.

A question to consider at this juncture is, "Does what happens to Israel have a typological fulfillment with the US?" They both are a land of unwalled villages; they both are at rest and dwell safely without walls; they both were once desolate places and are now inhabited by people gathered from all the nations of the world; they both are prosperous and have cattle, food, and goods in the middle sections of their land. I am not saying categorically that the Russian confederacy is going to come after the US to take a spoil, but I must admit, it is something I have wondered about. Reading Ezekiel 38:8-13 could engender such a question.

> 8After many days thou shalt be visited: in the latter years
> thou shalt come into the land that is brought back from
> the sword, and is gathered out of many people, against
> the mountains of Israel, which have been always waste:
> but it is brought forth out of the nations, and they shall
> dwell safely all of them. 9Thou shalt ascend and come
> like a storm, thou shalt be like a cloud to cover the land,
> thou, and all thy bands, and many people with thee.
> 10Thus saith the Lord GOD; It shall also come to pass, that
> at the same time shall things come into thy mind, and
> thou shalt think an evil thought: 11And thou shalt say, I
> will go up to the land of unwalled villages; I will go to
> them that are at rest, that dwell safely, all of them dwell-
> ing without walls, and having neither bars nor gates,
> 12To take a spoil, and to take a prey; to turn thine hand
> upon the desolate places that are now inhabited, and

> upon the people that are gathered out of the nations, which have gotten cattle and goods, that dwell in the midst of the land. [13]Sheba, and Dedan, and the merchants of Tarshish, with all the young lions thereof, shall say unto thee, Art thou come to take a spoil? Hast thou gathered thy company to take a prey? To carry awaysilver and gold, to take away cattle and goods, to take a great spoil?
> —Ezekiel 38:8-13

Verses 8 and 9 state that in the last days when Israel is dwelling safely, Gog with a vast army will come into the land of Israel, ascending like a storm. Verse 10 says that at the same time they do this, another thought will come into Gog's mind, and he shall think an evil idea. Gog will declare that he will go to the land of unwalled villages which were inhabited by a people gathered out of the nations to take a spoil. Other countries will question what his intentions are. I personally believe that the Battle of Gog and Magog will take place during the fourth seal of Revelation, chapter six. One-fourth of the world's population will die because of the four severe judgments – the sword, famine, pestilence, and the beasts. I say this to make the point that the world will be in short supply of the necessities of life and, therefore, be very motivated to take spoils from the wealthier nations. Again I am not suggesting this will definitely happen, but it is at least worth some consideration. Whatever you might think about the Battle of Gog and Magog, the widespread death and destruction, especially in the Islamic nations, will undoubtedly deter any other governments from challenging Israel and her God. The global turmoil might instead inspire them to adopt a spirit of unity instead of continuing the spirit of competition between nations. This could lead to a one-world government and a new world order. Could it also be that the results of this war will inspire this one-world government to make a peace treaty with Israel and redirect the blame for all the world's turmoil toward the Church instead? It would be good to do what the psalmist says, "SELAH" – (think about it).

CHAPTER 17

EMERGENCE OF THE BEAST

Introduction

John, the apostle, made very clear that one of the signs indicating the arrival of the last days would be the coming of the Antichrist – 1 John 2:18.

> 18Little children, it is the last hour; and as you have heard that the Antichrist is coming, even now many antichrists have come, by which we know that it is the last hour.
>
> —1 John 2:18

Revelation chapters 12 and 13 make it very clear that the emergence of the Beast and the Antichrist will take place before the catching away of the manchild and the beginning of the great tribulation. For more information about this, see chapters 13 and 14 of *The Terminal Generation* book.

I believe that the third and fourth seals set the stage and pave the way for this to happen. During the hyperinflation of the third seal, the economies of the world will spiral out of control, thus necessitating a one-world financial system and currency. Couple that with the devastating effects of the fourth seal where a fourth of the world's population die because of universal famine, natural disasters, anarchy, and pestilences, then you will have a prescription for political, social, and economic chaos. And add to that the battle of Gog and Magog, during which a confederacy of numerous Islamic nations have five-sixths of their armies annihilated in one day, and you create a need for a one-world government to usher in the new world order. The nations will not willingly choose to work together; instead, they will be forced to do so for their survival.

Though the great red dragon/beast will be in position at the time of the birth of the manchild, he won't be recognized as the Antichrist until after the manchild is caught up to heaven and the war between Michael and Satan is over. I believe the manchild is what keeps the Beast from being able to take his prophetic place in the world. After that which restrains is taken away, then he will be recognized as the invincible leader of this world. They will believe the strong delusion and be convinced that the Antichrist is actually God. Paul warns of this in 2 Thessalonians chapter two and Revelation chapter twelve.

> [6]And now you know what is restraining, that he may be
> revealed in his own time. [7]For the mystery of lawlessness

> is already at work; only He who now restrains will do so until He is taken out of the way. [8]And then the lawless one will be revealed, whom the Lord will consume with the breath of His mouth and destroy with the brightness of His coming. —2 Thessalonians 2:6-8

> [13]Now when the dragon saw that he had been cast to the earth, he persecuted the woman who gave birth to the male Child. [14]But the woman was given two wings of a great eagle, that she might fly into the wilderness to her place, where she is nourished for a time and times and half a time, from the presence of the serpent.
> —Revelation 12:13-14

Before I discuss the rise of the beast from the sea, I want to reiterate a point I referenced in *The Terminal Generation,* chapters 10 and following. What I am referencing is that John was commanded to write the story of what the future holds from approximately 95 AD to the Great White Throne Judgment and the eternal state. He began telling the story of the future in Revelation 4:1. The point I make is that the story of the future is articulated twice, first from a heavenly perspective and second from an earthly perspective. Chapter 12 ends the telling of the story from the heavenly perspective, and chapter 13 begins telling the same story from an earthly perspective. With this in mind, let us examine the dragon-empowered empire depicted in Revelation, chapters 12 and 13.

Rise and Revealing of the Beast

In verse one of Revelation 13, we see the rising of the beast from the sea.

> [1]Then I stood on the sand of the sea. And I saw a beast rising up out of the sea, having seven heads and ten horns, and on his horns ten crowns, and on his heads a blasphemous name. —Revelation 13:1

In verse eleven, we see the rise of the False Prophet from the earth, not from the sea like the Beast. What is the significance of the different origins of the two? Revelation 17:15 gives us a hint.

> [15]Then he said to me, "The waters which you saw, where the harlot sits, are peoples, multitudes, nations, and tongues. —Revelation 17:15

The waters being referred to in this verse are the seas which surround all the nations and peoples of the earth. This signifies that the Beast's emergence into a place of power and authority is of universal origin and dominion. Remember, the Beast not only refers to a worldwide empire but also its leader, the Antichrist. In the case of the False Prophet, however, the reference is to an individual who gives allegiance to the Antichrist and his empire. His origin is not from the whole world but a specific place on the earth; thus, his rise is not from the sea but from the earth.

Notice in Revelation 13 that when the Beast rises from the sea, he has seven heads, ten horns, and ten crowns

(7-10-10). In Revelation 12 the dragon has seven heads, ten horns, and seven crowns (7-10-7).

> [3]And another sign appeared in heaven: behold, a great, fiery red dragon having seven heads and ten horns, and seven diadems on his heads. —Revelation 12:3

Whereas chapter 13 shows the Beast's rise to power, chapter 12 depicts the satanically empowered Beast after his rise to power. Let us examine the discrepancy of the number of crowns or diadems on the heads of the ten horns in these two chapters. Most readers assume that the events of chapter 13 chronologically follow the events of chapter 12. They conclude that three more crowns were added to the seven after chapter twelve's conclusion. The real truth can be seen in comparing Daniel 7:7,8,19-27. Here we see that the little horn (Antichrist) was one of the ten horns who subdued three of the ten horns or leaders. There were still ten kingdoms (horns) but only seven rulers (crowns).

> [7]"After this, I saw in the night visions, and behold, a fourth beast, dreadful and terrible, exceedingly strong. It had huge iron teeth; it was devouring, breaking in pieces, and trampling the residue with its feet. It was different from all the beasts that were before it, and it had ten horns. [8]I was considering the horns, and there was another horn, a little one, coming up among them, before whom three of the first horns were plucked out by the roots. And there, in this horn, were eyes like the eyes of a man, and a mouth speaking pompous words.
>
> —Daniel 7:7-8

> [24]The ten horns are ten kings who shall arise from this kingdom. And another shall rise after them; he shall be different from the first ones and shall subdue three kings. [25]He shall speak pompous words against the Most High, shall persecute the saints of the Most High, and shall intend to change times and laws. Then the saints shall be given into his hand for a time and times and half a time. —Daniel 7:24-25

From these Scriptures we can see that the time frame where the Beast has seven crowns is a later development than when he had ten crowns. This proves, chronologically speaking, that the depiction of the satanic-empowered Beast recorded in chapter 12 is a later stage of development than that which is recorded in chapter 13. This further reinforces the fact that this chapter starts telling the story all over again from a natural or earthly perspective.

Mystery of the Heads and the Horns

When it comes to solving the mystery of what the seven heads of the Beast represent, the interpretation is not left to the reader. God gave His own explanation as to their meanings in Revelation, chapter seventeen.

> [8]The beast that you saw was, and is not, and will ascend out of the bottomless pit and go to perdition. And those who dwell on the earth will marvel, whose names are not written in the Book of Life from the foundation of the world, when they see the beast that was, and is not,

> and yet is. [9]"Here is the mind which has wisdom: The seven heads are seven mountains on which the woman sits. [10]here are also seven kings. Five have fallen, one is, and the other has not yet come. And when he comes, he must continue a short time. [11]The beast that was, and is not, is himself also the eighth, and is of the seven, and is going to perdition. [12]"The ten horns which you saw are ten kings who have received no kingdom as yet, but they receive authority for one hour as kings with the beast. [13]These are of one mind, and they will give their power and authority to the beast.
>
> —Revelation 17:8-11

The seven heads are seven mountains or empires and their respective seven kings who all play a significant role in the history and future of God's people. At the time of John's writing of the Revelation in 95 AD, five kings and their empires had already fallen. Those empires in order were the Egyptian empire, the Assyrian empire, the Babylonian empire, the Mede and Persian empire, and the Grecian empire. The sixth empire, of which John was a contemporary, was the Roman empire. The seventh empire and the king who was to come is the Antichrist who becomes the ruler of the entire realm of the Beast. This king will only rule but a short time.

The ten horns are ten future kings that one day will receive power and authority to rule, as the seventh beast emerges on the world scene prior to the great tribulation.

The Antichrist and His Mortal Wound

Now we will look at some other details mentioned in the above passage concerning the Antichrist. This passage says that he was and is not, and at a future time will ascend out of the bottomless pit. What does this mean? The phrase, "he was" signifies that he did exist. The phrase, "he is not" signifies that he stopped living because he died. The phrase, "he is" means that he who was dead exists again. How can this be? The answer is found in Revelation 13:3.

In this verse, John said he saw that one of the seven heads was mortally wounded, but then raised from the dead. As we shared earlier in the seventeenth chapter, this head or king was one of the seven leaders that becomes the eighth. I believe that the seventh king who is yet to come will rule but a short time, when most likely an assassination will take place. Personally, I think Satan will incarnate within his dead body, causing him to be raised from the dead. By so doing, Satan will have counterfeited the same storyline of the death and resurrection of Jesus Christ. There is nobody who should know better than Satan the compelling results of that storyline. Combine the Beast's being raised from the dead with all the supernatural powers of Satan working through him, and it leaves little to the imagination as to why everyone marvels over him and worships him and the dragon. The people of the earth will see him as being invincible, and none would be able to be victorious who would wage war against him. All whose names are not written in the Lamb's Book of Life will indeed worship him.

Characteristics of the Beast

Revelation 13:2 states that this beast will have traits like a leopard, a bear, and a lion. He will receive his power and great authority from Satan himself.

> [2]Now the beast which I saw was like a leopard, his feet were like the feet of a bear, and his mouth like the mouth of a lion. The dragon gave him his power, his throne, and great authority. —Revelation 13:2

This beast is depicted as being a composite of the first three beasts described in the vision found in the seventh chapter of Daniel.

> [2]Daniel spoke, saying, "I saw in my vision by night, and behold, the four winds of heaven were stirring up the Great Sea. [3]And four great beasts came up from the sea, each different from the other. [4]The first was like a lion, and had eagle's wings. I watched till its wings were plucked off, and it was lifted up from the earth and made to stand on two feet like a man, and a man's heart was given to it. [5]"And suddenly another beast, a second, like a bear. It was raised up on one side and had three ribs in its mouth between its teeth. And they said thus to it: 'Arise, devour much flesh!' [6]"After this I looked, and there was another, like a leopard, which had on its back four wings of a bird. The beast also had four heads, and dominion was given to it. [7]"After this, I saw in the night visions, and behold, a fourth beast, dreadful and terrible, exceedingly strong. It had huge iron teeth; it was devouring, breaking in pieces, and trampling the

> residue with its feet. It was different from all the beasts that were before it, and it had ten horns.
>
> —Daniel 7:2-7

As one compares the first three beasts with the fourth beast of Daniel 7:11-12, this passage seems to indicate that the first three beasts were contemporaries of the fourth. Even though they were not in power, yet they remained in existence for a short season even after the Beast was destroyed.

> 11"I watched then because of the sound of the pompous words which the horn was speaking; I watched till the beast was slain, and its body destroyed and given to the burning flame. 12As for the rest of the beasts, they had their dominion taken away, yet their lives were prolonged for a season and a time. —Daniel 7:11-12

As we look at the great image seen by Nebuchadnezzar in the dream recorded in Daniel, chapter two, we learn of the last five kingdoms of the seven that make up the seven heads of the Beast. The previous five empires in their chronological order are the Babylonians, the Medes & Persians, the Greeks, the Romans, and the Beast. The Egyptian and Assyrian empires had already come and fallen by the time of the reign of King Nebuchadnezzar, to whom the dream was given. One cannot help noticing the fact that there is no other "world empire" between the fall of the Roman Empire and the rise of the Empire of the Beast. However, there were notable dominant empires between these last two whose dominion spanned significant portions of the world. The vision of Daniel, chapter seven, speaks of these when it describes the lion with the eagle's wings, the bear, and the leopard with four heads and wings. The first represents the United Kingdom, which was weakened when the eagle's wings, representing the United States, were plucked from her dominion. The bear is represented by the USSR (Union of Soviet Socialist Republics). The leopard is represented by the German Empire who in thirty years seized dominion over vast portions of Europe and Africa on two different occasions.

Daniel 7:23 also indicates that which makes the fourth beast different from the other three beasts. It was that this one would devour the "whole world," tread it down, and break it in pieces.

> 23"Thus he said: 'The fourth beast shall be a fourth kingdom on earth, which shall be different from all other kingdoms, and shall devour the whole earth, trample it and break it in pieces. —Daniel 7:23

Could the United Nations eventually become the one-world government of this fourth beast? Let's take a closer look at this possibility.

The United Nations

The UN was formed on October 24, 1945, as a replacement for the ineffective League of Nations. It was established as an international peacekeeping organization to prevent another world war. This organization began with 51 nations and now numbers 193. The major players in its formation were the US, Soviet Union, England, China, and France. In particular, I want to bring to your attention the fact that the UN divided the world into 10 Regional Groupings. The post-World War II map was referred to as the "New World Order Map."

See http://nuclearsuntan.blogspot.com/ as a link to see the maps and peruse the information. Is it a coincidence that the empire of the Beast has ten horns and ten crowns? As I have stated in my book, *The Terminal Generation*, I believe the UN will be the one-world government eventually headed by the Antichrist. It will undoubtedly have more authority and power than it has now. The world will gladly give it such in the desperate times that are on the horizon.

CHAPTER 18

FEAST BETWEEN FEASTS

Introduction

Shortly after the emergence of the Antichrist, I believe the manchild of Revelation chapter twelve will be caught up to God without tasting death, as a firstfruits harvest to God and the Lamb. They will be changed in the twinkling of an eye. They will put on incorruption and immortality. This happens shortly before the great tribulation begins. Though I do not believe in a pre-trib rapture, I do believe in a rapture of the firstfruits redeemed from those living on the earth before the great tribulation. I am persuaded that Jesus will reap and wave this offering before His Father on the very day of Pentecost in the year this prophecy is fulfilled. Now let us look at this typological feast in more detail so that we might know better what to expect when the ultimate fulfillment takes place at the end of the age.

The Feast of Pentecost

This feast happens in Sivan, the third month of the sacred calendar. Sivan occurs from mid-May to mid-June on the Gregorian calendar. The feast gets its name from the transliteration of the Greek word, *Pentekostos*, which means "fiftieth." It is known by several other names, such as the Feast of Harvest (Exodus 23:16) and the Feast of Firstfruits (Numbers 28:26)(Exodus 23:16). It is also referred to as the Feast of Weeks (Exodus 34:22), with this name coming from the seven weeks plus one day (7x7+1 = 50) which separate the firstfruits of the barley and wheat harvests. Because it occurred after the offering of the firstfruits of Passover, it has acquired the name, "Feast of the Latter Firstfruits," which is vital to remember as we continue this study.

The Antitype of Pentecost

The feasts are all associated with the agricultural year and its various harvests. These are typological of the harvest of God's people which began shortly after Christ's resurrection and will conclude at the end of this age. Just as His people harvested their crops around these three festival seasons, God's Holy Days show us how He has and will harvest people for His kingdom.

Rain is a critical essential of harvest. Often prophecies about Pentecost describe this as an outpouring of rain. Rain is an invaluable ingredient of any successful harvest, no matter what crop we are talking about. Like natural rain, the pouring out of the Holy Spirit has to do with the birthing, maturing, and harvesting of God's people.

Whereas Passover was about the Seed dying and being planted in the earth, the Feast of Unleavened Bread was about the maturing of the fruit of that Seed, and the Feasts of Firstfruits and Pentecost were about the harvesting of the first ripened fruit of that Seed – John 12:23-24; Galatians 3:16.

> 23But Jesus answered them, saying, "The hour has come that the Son of Man should be glorified. 24Most assuredly, I say to you, unless a grain of wheat falls into the ground and dies, it remains alone; but if it dies, it produces much grain. —John 12:23-24

> 16Now to Abraham and his Seed were the promises made. He does not say, "And to seeds," as of many, but as of one, "And to your Seed," who is Christ.
>
> —Galatians 3:16

Earlier I discussed that Passover symbolized Christ's giving of Himself for us so our sins could be forgiven and we could be redeemed from death. I also shared how the Days of Unleavened Bread teach us that we must avoid and remove sin out of our lives. The next festival, Pentecost, builds on this important foundation.

It is believed that the law of Moses, the tabernacle order, the priesthood ministry, and the instructions for worship were given from Mt. Sinai on the Pentecost following Israel's deliverance from Egypt. However, the Bible emphatically states that by such law and external religion, no flesh shall be justified.

Humanly speaking, no matter how hard we try not to break the law, we still sin and fall short of God's glorious purpose – Romans 3:23. This purpose will never be realized by God's children while His laws remain written externally, on stone tablets or on the pages of a Bible. As it was in the beginning, so it is in the New Covenant. God's laws were, are now, and shall be written by His Spirit on the fleshly tablets of the hearts of men who partake of that New Covenant. Old Covenant typology speaks clearly as to where God initially intended His laws to abide. In the temple/tabernacle, the stone tablets were to reside in the ark of the covenant, which was in the Holy of Holies. In the New Covenant, we who have received the downpayment of the Holy Spirit baptism are the temples of God. Our spirit is the Holy of Holies of said temples, and this is where God writes His word and causes His laws to abide today. His laws are written and observed internally in the hearts of His children. Therefore, their worship migrates from being external to being internal. That which we were once oblivious to, we are no longer impervious to. Indeed the deadness of the letter of the law is swallowed up by the life of the spirit of the law.

The Two First-Fruits Offerings

It is important to remember that the most significant offerings could only be executed by the high priest. In all these offerings made to God, there must be three components.

What are these? They consist of God (the Receiver), a high priest who offers, and an offering that is given.

Now let us consider the antitype of the two firstfruits harvests of Passover and Pentecost and how they fit into God's prophetic timeline of these last days. We know that Jesus is the very firstfruits unto God of those who are raised from the dead, who put on incorruption and immortality. Though He is the first of His kind, He is not the only one of His kind.

> [52]and the graves were opened, and many bodies of the saints who had fallen asleep were raised; [53]and coming out of the graves after His resurrection, they went into the holy city and appeared to many.
>
> —Matthew 27:52-53

> [20]But now Christ is risen from the dead and has become the firstfruits of those who have fallen asleep. [21]For since by man came death, by Man also came the resurrection of the dead. [22]For as in Adam all die, even so in Christ, all shall be made alive. [23]But each one in his own order: Christ the firstfruits, afterward those who are Christ's at His coming. —1 Corinthians 15:20-23

Notice that these passages only speaks of the firstfruits of the dead. Christ resurrected first and then they who were resurrected the same day, as firstfruits unto God and the Lamb, followed after His resurrection. The main harvest of the righteous dead does not occur until the end of the age at the rapture.

> 15For this we say to you by the word of the Lord, that we
> who are alive and remain until the coming of the Lord
> will by no means precede those who are asleep. 16For
> the Lord Himself will descend from heaven with a shout,
> with the voice of an archangel, and with the trumpet of
> God. And the dead in Christ will rise first. 17Then we who
> are alive and remain shall be caught up together with
> them in the clouds to meet the Lord in the air. And thus
> we shall always be with the Lord.
>
> —1 Thessalonians 4:15-17

However, as stated above, the rapture is not just the main harvest of the righteous dead but also the righteous living. If the main harvest consists of two groups, there must be a firstfruit of both. The Bible supports the firstfruits from the grave after Christ is risen but are there any references to the firstfruits offering of those alive on the earth? Yes, as a matter of fact, there are more Scriptures concerning a firstfruit offering redeemed from those living on the earth than of those redeemed from their graves. I will list some of these for you below for your examination. I encourage you to read more about this in chapters 12-14 of my book, *The Terminal Generation*.

> 2And I heard a voice from heaven, like the voice of many
> waters, and like the voice of loud thunder. And I heard
> the sound of harpists playing their harps. 3They sang as
> it were a new song before the throne, before the four
> living creatures, and the elders; and no one could learn
> that song except the hundred and forty-four thousand
> who were redeemed from the earth. 4These are the

ones who were not defiled with women, for they are virgins. These are the ones who follow the Lamb wherever He goes. These were redeemed from among men, being firstfruits to God and to the Lamb.

—Revelation 14:2-4

1Now a great sign appeared in heaven: a woman clothed with the sun, with the moon under her feet, and on her head a garland of twelve stars. 2Then being with child, she cried out in labor and in pain to give birth. 3And another sign appeared in heaven: behold, a great, fiery red dragon having seven heads and ten horns, and seven diadems on his heads. 4His tail drew a third of the stars of heaven and threw them to the earth. And the dragon stood before the woman who was ready to give birth, to devour her Child as soon as it was born. 5She bore a male Child who was to rule all nations with a rod of iron. And her Child was caught up to God and His throne. 6Then the woman fled into the wilderness, where she has a place prepared by God, that they should feed her there one thousand two hundred and sixty days.

—Revelation 12:1-6

1Then I was given a reed like a measuring rod. And the angel stood, saying, "Rise and measure the temple of God, the altar, and those who worship there. 2But leave out the court which is outside the temple, and do not measure it, for it has been given to the Gentiles. And they will tread the holy city underfoot for forty-two months.

—Revelation 11:1-2

> 34"But take heed to yourselves, lest your hearts be weighed down with carousing, drunkenness, and cares of this life, and that Day come on you unexpectedly.
> 35For it will come as a snare on all those who dwell on the face of the whole earth. 36Watch therefore, and pray
> always that you may be counted worthy to escape all these things that will come to pass, and to stand before the Son of Man." —Luke 21:34-36

Notice that it is possible to escape all that was being spoken of earlier in the Olivet Discourse, such as the great tribulation and the wrath of God's judgment on the wicked. This last passage speaks of an overcoming group of saints who give themselves to watch and pray as they see the signs of the last days approaching. I believe these are the manchild of Revelation chapter twelve, the worshippers at the golden altar of Revelation eleven, and the firstfruits unto God and the Lamb of Revelation chapter fourteen. These are they who are caught up to God and His throne before the beginning of the tribulation period and the great day of God's wrath that take place the last seven years of this age.

Romans 8:29 speaks of Jesus Christ as "the firstborn of many brethren." The brethren represent the Church, who are considered to be firstfruits.

> 18Of His own will He brought us forth by the word of truth, that we might be a kind of firstfruits of His creatures. —James 1:18

Timing of the Two Firstfruits Offerings

When it comes to the timing of the offering of the firstfruits from the graves, we know it happened the morning after the Sabbath following the crucifixion of Jesus. This not only pinpoints the year but also the day of this offering. The year was the year of Christ's resurrection; the day was the Feast of Firstfruits of that same year. The timing of the second group is not so evident as the first. However, I do believe the feast during which the latter takes place is not ambiguous. As Jesus, the High Priest, waved the firstfruits from the grave on the Feast of the Firstfruits of the same year He came out of the tomb, I believe He will wave the latter firstfruits during the Feast of Pentecost of the same year before the great tribulation begins. I believe chapters eleven through fourteen of Revelation support the concept of separating a group to be spared from the great tribulation from a group who will go through it to be matured and cleansed.

Concerning the latter firstfruits, I would like to revisit Daniel's vision that I discussed in chapter three of this book. I believe there are clues there that give additional information as to the timing of this prophetic event.

Remember, Daniel sees a ram with two horns (Medes and Persians) being attacked and conquered by a he-goat with one notable horn (Greece led by Alexander the Great). Soon afterward, the large, notable horn (Alexander) dies. His kingdom is divided up into four regions and governed by his four notable generals.

I discussed the "two thousand three hundred-day time period" spoken of in Daniel 8:13-14. I believe it marks a span of time that begins with a leader taking over the empire of one of the four generals/notable horns. This successor will be the root that bears a branch which begins the genealogy that culminates with the birth of the Antichrist. This marks the beginning of the 2300-day prophecy. The end of this prophetic time period is characterized by the answer to a question that was asked in Daniel's dream. The question posed was, "When will this little horn stop the worship of God and trample God's children underfoot?" This is another way of asking, "When will the great tribulation begin?" "2300 days" was the answer given as to how long it would be from the initiating of that genealogy until the great tribulation. God's purpose for this tribulation will be the maturing and cleansing of His sanctuary. The sanctuary speaks of God's temple. God's temple in the last days refers to His church, not a reconstructed physical temple in Jerusalem.

Before continuing on with the speculation as to the meaning of the 2300 days, I want to interject a parenthetical identifying the four notable horns that rise up after Alexander's death. The importance of this information will be beneficial as we attempt to identify the little horn, the Antichrist, who is to come.

The Four Notable Horns

Typically when a ruler knew he was to die, they would name his successor. Most generally the oldest son was the choice. However, Alexander knew none of his heirs had the strength to continue his rule. When he was asked on his deathbed about who should succeed him, his reply was, "The Strongest." This led to a competitive group of generals vying for Alexander's empire. They are commonly referred to as, *The Diadochi*, which is the Greek word for "successors." Initially this included the likes of Ptolemy, Cassander, Lysimachus, and Antigonus I. Seleucus became governor of Babylon after Alexander died there. However, he had to flee to Egypt when opposed by Antigonus I, who because of his superior strength was on the verge of reuniting the Alexandrian empire under his sole leadership.

Desperate and jealous, Ptolemy, Cassander, and Lysimachus formed a coalition and went to war with him. Antigonus was killed in this war, and Seleucus began to rise in power as one of the four notable horns. However, Demetrius, the son of Antigonus I, eventually reclaimed part of his father's empire by replacing Cassander not too long after Cassander's death. After some years of infighting, post-Alexander, the four notable horns who finally emerged were Demetrius, Lysimachus, Seleucus, and Ptolemy. These became the fulfillment of Alexander's wishes to enthrone the strongest, as these proved to be the most powerful leaders who served under Alexander the Great. In 285 BC, Demetrius was forced to surrender to Seleucus and was imprisoned until his death in 283 BC. His son Antigonus II remained in charge of a portion of Demetrius' empire.

Eventually, Seleucus defeated and killed Lysimachus, ending his dynasty in 281 BC. And then three dynasties remained, and all of them had aspirations of reuniting the

Alexandrian empire under their sole leadership. From these three, we can determine that the Antichrist will come from one of the successors of Seleucus, Demetrius, or Ptolemy. Ptolemy is not an option because Daniel makes clear in chapter eleven that the Antichrist will one day attack Egypt, which is the origin of the Ptolemaic dynasty. Also in 281 BC, Ptolemy Keraunus murdered Seleucus. Seleucus' son, Antiochus II, succeeded him to the throne the same year. After Seleucus' death, Antigonus II, the son of Demetrius and grandson of Antigonus I, decided the time was ripe to take back his father's kingdom. He succeeded his father in 277 BC. With this information, I want to examine the meaning of the 2300 days spoken of in Daniel, chapter eight. From one of these (Antiochus II or Antigonus II) will come the Antichrist.

Significance of the 2300 Days

I now want to engage in some speculation as to the "Who" and "When" of this prophecy. I will base this educated guess on a combination of searching the Scriptures and history. If the Antichrist comes through a genealogy springing forth from one of the successors of the four generals, then knowing the year each one died and what year the one who successfully replaced them took the throne would aid us greatly in determining the timing of the great tribulation period's beginning.

From my personal studies, I believe there are only two possibilities as to who the little horn is that begins the genealogy that leads to the Antichrist. The two I speak of are

Antiochus II, the successor of Seleucus, or Antigonus II, the successor of Demetrius.

The successor is also known as the king of the North in Daniel 11:35-45. As I have said previously, the kings of the North and South and the boundaries of their kingdoms are determined by their directional proximity to Jerusalem. The leaders and the boundaries of their kingdoms changed so often throughout the ages that it becomes imperative that we take this into consideration when attempting to identify the "Who" and the "Where" of this end-time prophetic fulfillment. I personally believe that the nearest significant kingdom immediately North of Jerusalem at this present time would not be Lebanon but rather it is Turkey and its insignificant leader (the little horn).

Whoever this king of the North will be at the time of the fulfillment of this vision and wherever the boundaries of his kingdom will be, I do not know. I believe whoever he is, he will finally realize the dream of uniting the former Alexandrian empire under his sole leadership. It is prophesied about him that his real power will come after he usurps power over three of the ten horns/leaders of the empire of the Beast. After accomplishing this, he will be recognized as the supreme leader of the one-world government. He will be revered as the world's messiah and deliverer.

As to the timing of this prophetic event, I believe the 2300-day prophecy is as much a precise measuring tool as was the 70-week prophecy of Daniel. As we shared in Section 2 of this book, the 70-week prophecy was given so that Israel would know the exact time of their Messiah's arrival. In this prophecy, Israel knew that after the decree to rebuild Jerusalem until the coming of the Messiah would be 69 weeks or 483 years. Jesus' coming marked the beginning of the last (70th) week of Israel's age before the age of the Gentiles. Likewise, it is my opinion that from the appointed successor until the Antichrist's persecution of the saints in the great tribulation will be precisely 2300 years. If God gave such specific detail about the timing of His first appearing, why should we expect any less specific detail concerning the timing of His appearance at the end of this Gentile age?

If we know the year the two successors began their reigns and add 2300 years, we would know the timing of the start of the great tribulation. The two that I speak of are Antiochus II who succeeded Seleucus in 281 BC and Antigonus II who succeeded Demetrius in 277 BC. If you add 2300 years to each date, we get two possible starting dates for the great tribulation which are 2020 AD and 2024 AD. Again I want to remind you that I am not dogmatically stating that the tribulation will definitely begin in 2020 or 2024, but there is enough biblical support to at least prayerfully consider it as a possibility.

CHAPTER 19

Great Tribulation & Beyond

Introduction

In this last chapter I will very briefly cover all the major prophetic events that follow the beginning of the great tribulation, since I covered these in greater detail in *The Terminal Generation*. My primary goal is to map out what will happen before and up to the advent of the great tribulation. Once the tribulation starts, the time of preparation is over and gives way to a time of endurance for God's people throughout the first half of the last seven years of this age. The last three and a half years of this age are marked by God's supernatural protection and provision for His saints while He brings His judgments upon the inhabitants of the earth. The remaining events, from the rapture to the Great White Throne Judgment, will follow in succession as clearly articulated in the Scriptures.

The Great Tribulation

The Bible clearly and repeatedly defines the great tribulation as a period of three and a half years during which His church will be tested and purified. The Beast will receive authority to rule all the people and nations of the world. During his reign, he will blaspheme God, His name, His tabernacle, and all who dwell in heaven. It will be given unto him to make war against the saints of God and prevail against them for forty-two months. Nominal and genuine Christians will both be tested during this time, but only those who endure to the end will be saved. Some of God's people will love not their lives unto death and with unwavering faith will be martyred, receiving a better reward. Others will suffer many things for Jesus' namesake and endure all that the Antichrist and his beastly government will do to destroy the church of God. These, through much tribulation, will be caused to enter the kingdom of God while on the earth, as a mature, overcoming church. As concerning the timing of the great tribulation, it begins after the third and fourth seals/signs are completed. These seals are identified by Jesus as being the beginning of birth pains, which will lead to the birth and catching away of the firstfruits manchild of Revelation, chapter twelve.

The Day of the Lord

Immediately after the days of the great tribulation, the sun will be darkened, the moon will be turned to blood, and the sign of Christ's coming will be seen by all the inhabitants on the earth. This coming is not to be confused with His second coming when He comes to the earth on a white horse with His army of saints and angels. This particular coming is speaking about the sixth seal where He comes on a white throne to announce the pending judgments that will soon follow as judgment to the wicked. This announcement is so terrifying that men's hearts will fail them for fear of that which is about to happen. Many will actually cry out, asking the rocks to fall on and cover them to hide them from the face of Him who sits upon the throne.

After the sixth seal opens and before the seventh seal begins to unfold, the saints will be sealed with the mark of God on their foreheads. This seal will protect and insulate the church from the judgments of the seven trumpets/bowls prophesied to take place during the last three and a half years of this age.

Whereas the sixth seal is the announcement of the coming Day of the Lord's Wrath, the seventh seal is the actual unfolding of it. It is essential to understand that the Day of the Lord is not a literal day, but rather a period of time that begins immediately after the great tribulation and concludes 1335 days after the second coming of Jesus (see Daniel twelve study in chapter five of this book). At His coming, Jesus will complete His judgments at the battle of Armageddon and then establish His kingdom on the earth for one thousand years.

The Rapture

At the seventh trump, which is near the conclusion of the Day of the Lord, Jesus will descend from heaven and harvest all the believing souls ever conceived from Adam to the sounding of that seventh trumpet. This includes all believers who have died and those who are alive at that time. This is the first resurrection, at which time our corruptible mortal bodies will put on incorruption and immortality. This coming of the Lord is not to be confused with coming before the Day of the Lord or His second coming when He actually touches down on the earth at the Mt. of Olives and engages the armies of the world who are gathered around Jerusalem at the battle of Armageddon. At the rapture, Christ descends as His harvested saints meet Him in the air to forever be with Him. He does not proceed with His saints to the earth but instead takes His bride back to heaven to present her to His Father.

The Judgment Seat of Christ

Immediately after the rapture, the saints stand before God at the Judgment Seat of Christ to be judged for their works on earth and receive rewards according to the quality of those works. Like the rapture, this event also takes place during the seventh and last trumpet, as recorded in Revelation 11:18.

> 18The nations were angry, and Your wrath has come, and the time of the dead, that they should be judged, and that You should reward Your servants the prophets and

> the saints, and those who fear Your name, small and great, and should destroy those who destroy the earth."
>
> —Revelation 11:18

It is the judgment of the righteous who lived prior to and up to the rapture. This judgment is not about personal "identity" but rather personal "achievement." It's not about whether you are a believer or nonbeliever, but rather the quality of your works as a believer. This judgment is not to determine our eternal destination (heaven or hell) but rather the quality of it. We should not look at the judgment seat of Christ as God judging our sins, but rather as God judging our works. Its purpose is to reward His children for their faithful works done while on earth.

> [11]For no other foundation can anyone lay than that which is laid, which is Jesus Christ. [12]Now if anyone builds on this foundation with gold, silver, precious stones, wood, hay, straw, [13]each one's work will become clear; for the Day will declare it, because it will be revealed by fire; and the fire will test each one's work, of what sort it is. [14]If anyone's work which he has built on it endures, he will receive a reward. [15]If anyone's work is burned, he will suffer loss; but he himself will be saved, yet so as through fire. —1 Corinthians 3:11-15

Not only is this judgment to reward the saints for their good works, but also to purge them of substandard works that would defile them and thereby disqualify them from entering the presence of the Lord – Revelation 21:27.

> 27But there shall by no means enter it anything that defiles, or causes an abomination or a lie, but only those who are written in the Lamb's Book of Life.
>
> —Revelation 21:27

The Marriage

Once the saints are refined through the fires of the judgment of the Bema Seat, Christ will present them to His Father without spot or blemish. What follows is the marriage of the Lamb of God to His bride. For more details concerning this heavenly event, read chapter twenty-seven of *The Terminal Generation*. All saints who comprise the bride and those attending the wedding and marriage supper as friends of the bride or groom will be appropriately attired in holy wedding garments.

The Second Coming

What happens after the marriage supper? As was often customary, the Bridegroom will take His Bride on a trip back to the former habitation of the Bride (the earth) to officially declare the consummation of their marriage to the people in the place of her former residence. It is the people and place where He and His lordship had been rejected earlier. This time the whole earth will know that He was and is the King of kings and Lord of lords. They will understand that He is truly the Son of God and that His wife, the Church, is His chosen bride (His Queen) who will rule and reign with Him over the entire earth.

This coming to the earth with His saints after the marriage feast is referred to theologically as the "Second Coming of Christ." At this coming, He will descend out of heaven on a white horse followed by His armies on their white horses. He and His armies will touch down on the Mount of Olives where all the armies of all the nations of this world will have gathered to destroy Israel and the holy city of Jerusalem. Throughout the ages, the devil has put into the hearts of men an obsession to exterminate Israel, the chosen nation of God, and to control and inhabit the city of Jerusalem. Even today, we hear the rhetoric of numerous countries with this obsession going unchallenged by the nations of this world. Where is the outrage? Would the nations who are silent find this rhetoric acceptable if they were the targets of such hatred? I don't think so! However, the Second Coming will be a day of the vengeance of our God upon all the nations for atrocities committed against God's chosen people. It will mark the culmination of three and one-half years of the judgment referred to as "the great day of God's wrath." This coming is a part of the judgment of the seventh trumpet/bowl. The surviving Jews will recognize that the promised Messiah is the very Jesus they had rejected. They will become believers and, in fact, will be the only believers here on earth that are yet in natural bodies. These will join with the Lord and His armies to fight and prevail against the armies of this world in that great battle called Armageddon. The Lord will use this battle, as well as the other previous judgments, to deliver the earth of its most vile influences. After this battle, the Lord will capture the Beast and the False Prophet and cast them alive into the Lake of Fire so they no longer can negatively influence and deceive the inhabitants of this earth. The devil, however, will be taken, chained, and cast into the bottomless pit for a thousand years, that he would not be able to deceive the nations any more until the end of the thousand years.

We, the saints, will be here to rule and reign with Christ in our glorified bodies for a thousand years. The "Elect Remnant" of Israel that is now saved will be established as a kingdom of priests to this earth. They will accept the very priesthood they rejected in Moses' day. They, as priests who have access to God, will minister to those earthlings who do not yet have access to God. Through their priesthood, the salvation of God will be extended to the unbelievers who survived to enter the millennial reign of Christ.

The Millennial Kingdom

The millennial kingdom is the restoration of the Edenic State (Garden of Eden) on this earth. Once again peace, prosperity, health, longevity, joy, rejoicing, holiness, absence of the curses (i.e., thorns, thistles, weeds, pestilences, poisonous snakes, etc.) are all re-established on the earth – Micah 4:1-5; Isaiah 11:5-10; Isaiah 32:13-18; Zechariah 14:8-11. Eden was a mix of both natural and supernatural trees. It was the intersection of the kingdom of heaven with the natural, earthly kingdom.

In the beginning, God gave the dominion to rule over this earth to man under God's divine headship. Man abdicated this charge, and Satan usurped man's God-given role. For six millenniums, God has tolerated the mismanagement of this earth by man and Satan. God's purposed plan from the beginning will finally find its fulfillment during the seventh millennium. Christ will establish His rule and reign on the earth for one thousand years. He once again will give to mankind that portion of God's authority, which is the earth.

At the end of the millennium, He will loose the devil out of the bottomless pit for a short season to once again deceive, tempt, and influence those who are not the true worshippers of God.

However, those who worship God only externally will be influenced and led astray by the devil at the end of the age. They will unite with him, pledge allegiance to him, and will enlist in the devil's army in an attempt to overthrow the nation of Israel. This will culminate in that great and final battle called Gog and Magog in which the devil and his massive army will surround and fight against the saints of God and the city of Jerusalem. This is not to be confused with the Gog and Magog battle of Ezekiel 38-39 which occurs prior to the great tribulation.

> 7 Now when the thousand years have expired, Satan will
> be released from his prison 8 and will go out to deceive
> the nations which are in the four corners of the earth,
> Gog and Magog, to gather them together to battle,
> whose number is as the sand of the sea. 9 They went up
> on the breadth of the earth and surrounded the camp
> of the saints and the beloved city. And fire came down
> from God out of heaven and devoured them. 10 The
> devil, who deceived them, was cast into the lake of fire

> and brimstone where the beast and the false prophet are. And they will be tormented day and night forever and ever. —Revelation 20:7-10

God will utterly destroy His opposers by sending down fire from heaven. He will cast the devil into the Lake of Fire where the Beast and False Prophet are to be tormented day and night forever and ever.

The Great White Throne Judgment

Immediately following this second battle of Gog and Magog, God will appear on a great white throne to bring His final judgment on this earth and its inhabitants, whether they be spirit beings or human beings. All of mankind that was not a part of the Bema Seat judgment will stand before God to be judged out of the books of the Bible. They will be judged for the works they did while in their mortal bodies. Just as there are degrees of rewards for the saints for their works, so shall there also be degrees of everlasting punishment for unbelievers for their works.

> [13]" Woe to you, Chorazin! Woe to you, Bethsaida! For if the mighty works which were done in you had been done in Tyre and Sidon, they would have repented long ago, sitting in sackcloth and ashes. [14]But it will be more tolerable for Tyre and Sidon at the judgment than for you. —Luke 10:13-14

It seems people will have to answer for all the opportunities God gave them throughout their lives to receive His grace – the greater the opportunity, the greater the accountability. Jesus taught that to whom much is given, much is required. This part of the judgment has nothing to do with a person's eternal destination. It merely determines the quality of either destination.

> [11]Then I saw a great white throne and Him who sat on it, from whose face the earth and the heaven fled away. And there was found no place for them. [12]And I saw the dead, small and great, standing before God, and books were opened. And another book was opened, which is the Book of Life. And the dead were judged according to their works, by the things which were written in the books. [13]The sea gave up the dead who were in it, and Death and Hades delivered up the dead who were in them. And they were judged, each one according to his works. [14]Then Death and Hades were cast into the lake of fire. This is the second death. [15]And anyone not found written in the Book of Life was cast into the lake of fire.
>
> —Revelation 20:11-15

It is interesting to note that the grave and hell will deliver up all the dead within them, and all (100 percent) will be cast into the lake of fire, which is the second death. Concerning those who are alive when this judgment takes place, they too will be judged. Some will go to the left as goats and some to the right as sheep. Whoever is not found written in the Lamb's Book of Life will be cast into the Lake of Fire. Those whose names are written in the Book will enter into the joy of God's rest to forever be with the Lord God.

The Eternal State

And then time will be no more. Only the "eternal state" will exist. In the eternal state, God will bring many changes to what mankind has known on this earth. Eternity is a never-ending present tense. Some will inherit eternal life, which is a never-ending union with the Great "I AM" where the past and future no longer exist. Unbelievers will inherit eternal death, which is a never-ending separation from the presence of God. These will not be consumed in the fire or cease to exist, as some teach. Jesus describes this judgment as everlasting punishment and torments.

However, significant changes will be a first-time experience for those who inherit eternal life. One change will be a doing away with the old and the bringing in of the new. The old heavens and earth will pass away, and God will make a new heaven and new earth – Revelation 21:1-5. The new earth will have no seas. Imagine the entire globe without any oceans or seas. There will be no sun or moon to light it. The glory of God will illuminate the new earth. Night/darkness will be no longer, because His glory will always be the light of it.

There will be no more tears, death, sorrow, crying, nor pain. All these former things will pass away and be replaced with the loving, glorious presence of the Living God forever.

> 3And I heard a loud voice from heaven saying, "Behold, the tabernacle of God is with men, and He will dwell with them, and they shall be His people. God Himself

> will be with them and be their God. [4]And God will wipe away every tear from their eyes; there shall be no more death, nor sorrow, nor crying. There shall be no more pain, for the former things have passed away
>
> —Revelation 21:3-4

The testimony of this last book of the Bible ends with a loving invitation to "Come" to experience that which God has prepared for those who love Him.

And finally, in verse 21 we see once again the prophet fast forwards to the very end of the day of the Lord when Israel is surrounded by the armies of all the nations of the world. Zephaniah declares that at that time, half of the city of Jerusalem will have fallen and two-thirds of the Jews will have died. When all hope of survival seems to be gone for the remaining Jews who are trapped in the city, then suddenly God intervenes. Obadiah says that saviors shall come to Mt. Zion to judge those who are gathered on the mountains of Esau, and the kingdom shall be the Lord's. This is speaking of the second coming of Jesus, the Savior, with His saints, the saviors, to destroy the armies at Armageddon. Then the kingdoms of this world will become the kingdoms of our Lord and of His Christ, and He shall reign forever and ever! It is at this time that the King of kings will establish His millennial reign on the earth and Israel will once again be the focus of God's love and the delight of the earth.

> [21]Then saviors shall come to Mount Zion to judge the mountains of Esau, and the kingdom shall be the LORD's.
>
> —Obadiah 1:21

WE SHALL RULE

AND REIGN WITH HIM

ON THIS EARTH

FOR

ONE THOUSAND YEARS.

AND THEN,

TIME WILL BE NO MORE.

APPENDIX A

Syria
Lebanon
West Bank
Gaza Strip
Jordan
Iraq
Iran
Kuwait
Egypt
Saudi Arabia
Bahrain
Qatar
UAE
Sudan

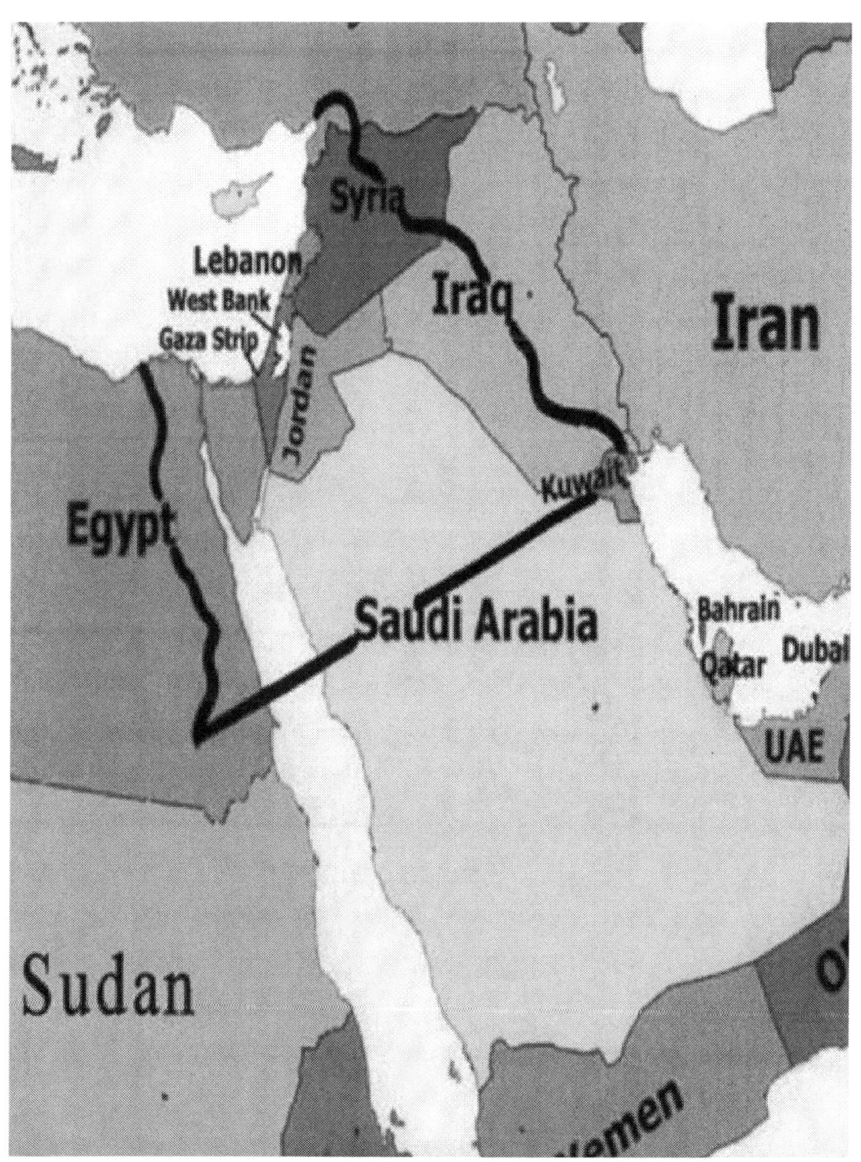

APPENDIX B

Timeline

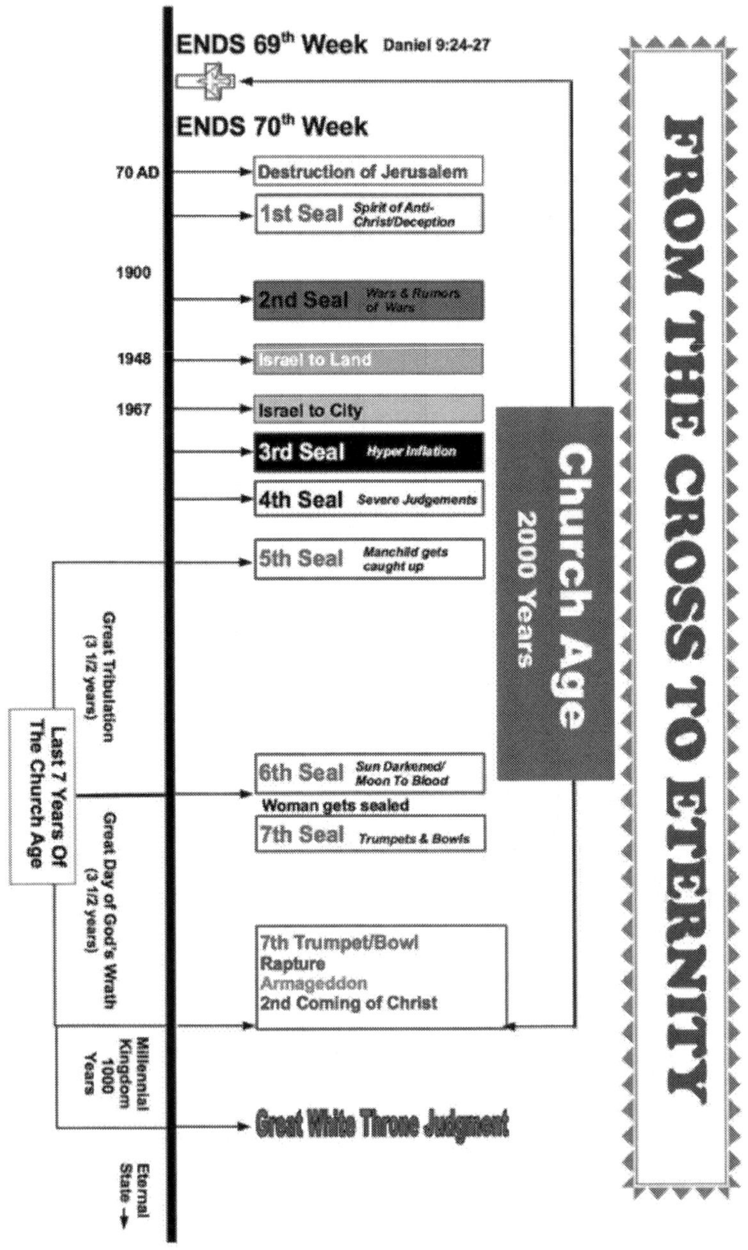

Made in the USA
Lexington, KY
14 September 2019